KU-184-707

Pushkin in 1827

Leslie O'Bell

PUSHKIN'S
EGYPTIAN
NIGHTS

The Biography of a Work

ARDIS /// ANN ARBOR

Copyright © 1984 by Ardis Publishers

All rights reserved.
Printed in the United States of America.
No part of this publication may be reproduced, stored in a retrieval system or transmitted in any form or by any means, electronic, mechanical, photocopying, recording, or otherwise, without the prior permission of the publisher.

Ardis Publishers
2901 Heatherway
Ann Arbor, Michigan 48104

ISBN 0-88233-925-7

Library of Congress Cataloging in Publication Data

O'Bell, Leslie.
    Pushin's "Egyptian Nights".

    Bibliography: p.
    1. Pushkin, Aleksandr Sergeevich. 1799-1837. Egipetskie
nochi.   2. Cleopatra, Queen of Egypt, d. 30 B.C., in
fiction, poetry, drama, etc.   I. Title.
PG3323.E3302   1983   891.71'3   83-22396
ISBN 0-88233-925-7

For my parents and for Donald

CONTENTS

PREFACE

This book follows one literary conception over the career of a great writer, the Cleopatra theme in Pushkin. It starts with the famous poem and ends with the story "Egyptian Nights." All of the works which it treats are fragments, some deliberately so, others clearly unfinished. Yet all of them also have an astonishing imaginative potency; in their brevity they seem more and not less significant, open-ended rather than closed. They fairly leap off the page. At least one of them did for Tolstoy. On opening his Pushkin at random he happened to read "The guests gathered at the dacha," the first line of one prose fragment. "There is the way to begin," he marveled. And with that *Anna Karenina* was launched.

To a Russian every line of Pushkin is dear, and Pushkin scholarship has often worried to death the smallest details of his work. Yet the master's hand is indeed apparent in all that Pushkin touches. Probably equal sensitivity is demanded not to trivialize a spacious masterpiece like *Eugene Onegin* or a lyric in its smaller perfection. There is a kind of critical snobbery which prefers the smaller forms in art to the cumbersome "war-horses": chamber music to the symphony, sketches to the canvas in oils, anything to the novel. That attitude had nothing to do with the writing of this book. The Cleopatra fragments are ultimately rewarding because they call on the reader to integrate a great deal of Pushkin in order to appreciate them. They are significant because they form a series that bridges the major moments in Pushkin's career, brings out his scope as a writer and mirrors his development. In this they are unique. No other conception exists which unfolds Pushkin to us in this way, not even *Onegin* itself. If the fragments show less of the result they show more of the process of literary creation, the real center of this study. What we see, then, is not a tiny corner of Pushkin's world but a sidelong view of the whole. The fragments considered this way also afford that highest of intellectual pleasures, the perception of unity in diversity.

They do show to greatest advantage a relatively unfamiliar side of Pushkin. Cleopatra has been called the "anti-Tatyana." If Tatyana was Pushkin's muse, then Cleopatra was a sort of anti-muse. It is no wonder that her figure accompanied Pushkin for so long. There used to be a popular notion of "two Pushkins," the poet and the man (a division of roles which "Egyptian Nights" tends to substantiate). The idea needs considerable refinement, and I am not concerned to write Pushkin's biography here. However, even as a writer Pushkin is at least two-fold. Roughly speaking, there is Pushkin the progenitor of *War and Peace* and Pushkin the progenitor of *Anna Karenina*. The first is historically minded, realist, optimistic; the second is also plagued by all the complexes of modern man, full of symbolic image, even demonic. The second Pushkin is more prominent in this study. The Cleopatra fragments in fact dramatize a state of psychological dividedness with an ambivalence that defied resolution. Now critical tradition has a remedy for the divided Pushkin—the idea of his gradual and triumphant overcoming of romanticism. However, to understand the mature Pushkin I believe that we must give up thinking of him in stages. Style concepts do not march forward in his work like the periods of Marxist historical-economic development. In the end they become more like different stylistic languages used for different aims in different circumstances. Probably the notion of dialogue is more productive. Perhaps, after all, realism is only interesting when it is still in tension with the romantic imagination. In any case, there is no cause for surprise if "romantic" elements persist into late Pushkin, as they do in "Egyptian Nights." The latest Soviet scholarship has returned to acknowledging that Pushkin assimilates the accomplishments of romantic prose, and that "Egyptian Nights," in its lyricism somewhat exceeds the rather austere limits imposed by him on his prose style.

Exploring the creative history of the Cleopatra cycle led me to certain discoveries of a specific nature: the genesis of the Cleopatra poem, the notion of a general conversation and of a "conversationalist" in the development of the prose, the unity of "Egyptian Nights" in its double theme of Cleopatra and the poets, not to mention the interweaving of each fragment in the resilient fabric of Pushkin's work. But such originality as the book possesses derives from a wider attitude which I share with others: we must look for Pushkin's deeper and unifying structures of image and idea. However, the book is not a contribution to structuralism or any other theory in the abstract. It centers instead on Pushkin's creative thought and the ways through which it takes shape artistically. I ask the reader to follow in some detail the development of an ever larger associative complex, the cycle built on the original Cleopatra poem. This takes us from the semantic aura of a word to the representative realms of world culture and involves us in the old and honorable quarrel of ancients and moderns. The exercise is valuable if it conveys a practical experience of just what it means to say that a writer like Pushkin is capable of raising the particular to the universal.

Let me call on Dostoevsky for a postscript. In approaching Pushkin's Cleopatra we may encounter prudery on the one hand and the school-boy snicker on the other. The challenge is to find an authentic response so as to escape the withering reproach: "We are puritans by blood; we have little love for life, and therefore art seems to us a form of temptation." Pushkin started with striking and even sensational material, but the story of its artistic embodiment takes on a drama all its own.

PUSHKIN'S "EGYPTIAN NIGHTS"

THE BIOGRAPHY OF A WORK

INTRODUCTION

Pushkin's late and unfinished story, "Egyptian Nights," seems to have been left to posterity as a tantalizing riddle which defies complete solution. First of all, the story poses an unanswered question by means of a classical anecdote. We hear how the proud and bored Cleopatra challenges any of her admirers to claim a night of her love but to forfeit his life in the morning. Three come forward in readiness, but there is no account of the outcome of their bargain. What would really have become of them? Moreover, the Egyptian nights of antiquity have also been projected into the Russian present. The story asks by implication whether there exists in modern Petersburg a woman to equal Cleopatra, and more importantly, whether there still live men bold enough to accept her challenge. The classical anecdote is presented in verse form, while the modern situation frames it in prose, one fragment enclosing the other. Years later, the open questions inspired the symbolist Valery Bryusov to complete the poem "Cleopatra" and led his contemporary M. Hofman to devise an independent ending for the prose.[1] Not suprisingly, both sequels were more creations of the modernist period than extensions of Pushkin's work.

The aim of the present study is not to finish "Egyptian Nights." We are powerless to say how the work would have ended; most probably with one of Pushkin's characteristic twists. It is equally fruitless to speculate why the story of 1835 was never completed, remembering how many fragments, sketches and plans Pushkin left behind him at his untimely death in January, 1837. The story was not *a priori* doomed or flawed. It is permissible, however, to consider the alternatives implied in it and to ask how the choices came to be framed in Pushkin's terms.

As his first biographer wrote:

The impression produced by "Egyptian Nights" is so complete and so forceful that it must arouse to inquiry the reader who wishes to come to terms with his feelings. Anyone who has examined attentively this short but exemplary work must surely have noticed that all of its colors and all of its outlines have been thought out in an extraordinarily profound way, have been most rigorously weighed and evaluated beforehand, and only later reproduced at a moment of inspiration which imparts to

3

all of them the freshness and brilliance of a first impression. The story of the creation of "Egyptian Nights" is truly of this nature.[2]

The Cleopatra theme in fact had a remarkable tenacity of life within Pushkin's evolving work. He returned to the idea for "Egyptian Nights" or kindred ideas over a period of more than ten years. Even the writing of *Onegin* had not preoccupied him for so long, although it had done so more sustainedly, with fewer pauses and to greater result. In 1824 Pushkin composed "Cleopatra," the original version of the poem which figures in "Egyptian Nights." In 1828 he revised it and also wrote the first in a series of prose fragments which frame the poetic material, "The Guests Gathered at the Dacha." In 1830 he returned briefly to that fragment. This is the pre-history of the later developments of 1835. In 1833, however, a Cleopatra anecdote appeared in a different setting, the "Tale from Roman Life," also known as "Caesar was Traveling." Work on this fragment was renewed in January of 1835 but soon broken off. The Cleopatra anecdote was then recast into a story related to "Guests," "Evening at the Dacha"; at the same time the poem "Cleopatra" again underwent revision, this time rather extensively. Finally, the idea of "Cleopatra" was absorbed by a new one, "Egyptian Nights"—these are alternative titles for the last story of this cycle. Another productive line was now grafted onto the old material, namely an artist story concerning a pair of poets, Charsky and the Italian improvisor, a line which has its own genealogy.

The present study traces the creative history of "Egyptian Nights" which lies behind the bare outline just sketched, motivates the series of events, and does so as far as possible in terms of Pushkin's artistic work and thought. While respecting the individuality of the various literary conceptions as they arise and not contaminating one with another, it integrates them into a cycle. It also interprets the place which the cycle occupies when read in the larger picture of Pushkin's entire work. What results could be termed the critical biography of "Egyptian Nights." In order to establish it, the texts are analyzed into their component motifs and themes, whose lines of development and paths of convergence are followed. The approach makes use of a flexible notion of synonymy or equivalencies. For instance, the figure of the Italian improvisor is crucial to "Egyptian Nights," but other characters play an analogous role before he is invented. This reading is supplemented by a series of cross-sections of Pushkin's manuscripts. These sections are taken at every stage in the Cleopatra series and serve to bring out the flow of artistic impulses which influenced the appearance of each. For purposes of the present reading, drafts and variants which show the creative process can be as instructive as polished texts. Where fragments are concerned, the chief danger to interpretation lies in using too narrow an approach. Fragments are by nature potential works which require to be expanded upon if their general import is to be made clear. The natural approach to them is what is known as creative history.

Creative history appeared in the 1920's from the old historical-genetic school of criticism and was first championed by Piksanov in his studies of Griboedov.[3] Known in Europe as *Entstehungsgeschichte* or *critique de genèse*, it was a notable advance on the practice of influence-hunting. During the years of Marxist debate in Soviet aesthetics the approach appealed to those who put an emphasis on ideas and historical evolution as well as to those interested in the so-called literary fact, or literature as production. Creative history sometimes ventured then into the speculative realm of the artist's psychology. Recently it has borne fruit in Meylakh's book *Pushkin's Artistic Thinking as a Creative Process* (1962). The title is indicative: artistic thought as a process. The present study takes the works as central rather than the act of writing; that is, the aim is chiefly to interpret *what* Pushkin wrote as an evolving entity and not to generalize about how he wrote. Thus, it concerns more the history of the writer's creation than the nature of his creativity.

Where the history of the work is concerned, textologists are often of more help than the practitioners of creative history as such. As early as the 1930's Bondi formulated the need for a dynamic and not exclusively normative reading of Pushkin's manuscripts. They should be seen, he said, not as static results but as the reflection of a process unfolding in time. To rediscover this unfolding was to follow the flow of a writer's thought.[4] In Likhachev's words, thus is textual criticism raised from an auxiliary, editorial skill to an independent discipline which studies the emergence of works in context.[5] It is no surprise that some of the most illuminating studies of Pushkin's works in their creative development have been written by textologists.[6] More unorthodox but also more suggestive are the intuitive essays of twentieth-century poets like Khodasevich and Akhmatova.[7] Akhmatova, in particular, had a kind of genius for reading between the works. Bondi, as a textologist in the traditional sense of the word, spoke of a method required by drafts and manuscripts. Structuralism has widened the contemporary conception of text in such a way that it is now possible to regard the

5

work of a writer as a single "text" integrated into its literary and cultural "con-texts." The subject of the present study, then, could be called the Cleopatra text in Pushkin.

Indeed, closer acquaintance with "Egyptian Nights" almost compels the reader to broaden his idea of text. The very editorial history of the work puts us in the thick of its creative history. The story has appeared in different forms to different generations, and each version has been hypothetical and interpretive. The work read today remains an editorial reconstruction. Fair copy is available as far as the prose sections of the story are concerned, but the verse is another matter. The Cleopatra poem was introduced into the tale in the first place because the original editors of "Egyptian Nights" assumed, reasonably enough, that Pushkin intended some prepared verse segment to fill the gap which he left in the manuscript for the performance of the Italian improvisor. The Cleopatra improvisation appears there in its 1828 version, even though Pushkin had been in the course of recasting it in 1835 for a related fragment. From the editorial standpoint, the text cannot be otherwise, since Pushkin's reworking was not taken far enough to yield a continuous text. Another improvisation about the poet and the crowd makes its appearance only with the advent of twentieth-century editions, and then in two versions. The new editors concluded that Pushkin had destined for another ellipsis certain stanzas reworked in 1835 from the unfinished "Ezersky." A cumulative reading, like this one, does not aim at establishing a new edition of "Egyptian Nights" but rather at interpreting the story in light of the directions in which it was moving.

The fragments themselves became available to readers gradually. In the year of Pushkin's death, 1837, "Egyptian Nights" was published posthumously in *The Contemporary*. The story presented the text of the 1828 "Cleopatra" which for a long time to come remained the only version known to the public. Then Annenkov published several important fragments of the cycle in his book *Materials for a Biography of Pushkin* (1855) and also in the supplementary volume of his Pushkin edition (1857). These included parts of "Guests," of "Evening at the Dacha" and of the "Tale from Roman Life." Yakushkin was responsible for printing additional pieces of the puzzle in *Russian Heritage* for 1884 ("Guests," "Evening"). At the same time he also published most of the 1824 "Cleopatra." In 1882, Bartenev made available the 1835 "Cleopatra" as part of "Evening at the Dacha." But the study of textology and in particular of Pushkin's original manuscripts made great advances in the early twentieth century. Beginning with the 1920's, the text of "Egyptian Nights" was re-examined for Soviet editions. In 1931, Bondi's essay "Towards the History of the Creation of 'Egyptian Nights'" appeared in his *New Pages of Pushkin*,[8] with the aim of establishing a more accurate chronology and taking the first steps toward a creative history. The Pushkin Jubilee edition (1937-49) reproduced for the first time many drafts and variants connected with the cycle. However, the text contained there is not definitive; the latest editions incorporate corrections suggested by Tomashevsky in a 1955 article on the text of the poem "Cleopatra."[9]

Just as the publication of the Cleopatra cycle progressed by stages separated in time, so, too, the appreciation of it. The basic stages of critical interest in "Egyptian Nights" fall first in the 1850's, the period of the Pushkin revival, then in the 1880's leading into the symbolist period, and finally, in the 1920's and 30's, the time of the "overcoming of symbolism" in criticism as well as in literature. Annenkov was the first to set the critical orientation towards "Egyptian Nights"; Bryusov then established his influential interpretation; Tomashevsky and others have labored to recover Cleopatra's original significance. Annenkov wrote of the "strong romantic effect" which Pushkin meant to draw from the clash of ancient and modern values in the story; Bryusov of its symbolic correspondences, Tomashevsky of the poem's psychological paradox and historical insight—more Pushkin the realist than Pushkin the romantic or symbolist.

To date, the interpretation of the cycle as a whole has not equalled the efforts expended to establish its text. Despite his new ideal for textology, Bondi worked with a rather narrow notion of what constituted the history of "Egyptian Nights," excluding from it both "Guests" and the "Tale from Roman Life." Two other studies of the cycle exist, articles by Gorlin (1939) and Chirpak-Rozdina (1973),[10] but each is governed by a particular interest. Gorlin concentrates on 1834-35, impelled by the discovery of a parallel to Pushkin's "Evening at the Dacha" in Jules Janin's *roman frénétique*, *Barnave*. Chirpak-Rozdina comes close to creative history, but her treatment is spotty and her conclusions are marred by the desire to explain why Pushkin did not finish "Egyptian Nights."[11] The present study attempts to provide the missing overview and to penetrate far enough into the dynamic of Pushkin's work to show what underlying processes carried the Cleopatra conception forward from stage to stage. The tenacity of life possessed by the Cleopatra theme stems from the fact that it does not occupy an idiosyncratic or eccentric place in Pushkin's work. It offered a focus for important psychological, social and aesthetic problems.

As Tomashevsky justly remarked, creative history cannot be expected to answer all the "cursed questions."[12] But Likhachev was also right in saying that it could budge long-held critical stereotypes.[13] Soviet producers once worked on a film about Pushkin where a magic pen could be seen composing the *Bronze Horseman* word by word,[14] a critic's dream, since this is one of the few works all of whose manuscripts have survived. We rarely have the materials for such a dramatic and graphic demonstration, yet, as Tomashevsky put it, using a few salient points we can still draw a line.[15] Creative history is not an end in itself. The facts must always be accounted for critically, going both deep and wide: deep to penetrate the powers of language and wide to encompass many contexts of meaning.[16] Creative history is usually reserved for extensive masterpieces, macrocosms seen as the culmination and fulfillment of a writer's work. But it is also enlightening to reverse the perspective and view the whole through a microcosm.

This brings us squarely up to the problem of "the whole." Perhaps there is no such thing; perhaps there are only the separate works and the author's "work" is a critical fiction. Yet to glimpse this ideal entity is the ultimate object in reading a writer: we wish to know Pushkin, for the sake of his individual masterpieces, of course, but also because he is Pushkin, something greater than the sum of those parts. Pushkin is notoriously protean; still, other generations tried to grasp and fix him in his biographical double or in his emergent world-view or in the very cadence of his verse. Today we can also seek to integrate his text. Current studies of Pushkin's "poetic mythology" are one step in this direction.[17]

Tomashevsky was cautious about creative history but deeply knowledgeable about Pushkin's texts. He once wrote that "individual conceptions of various works are usually inseparable in a writer's creative life." You watch the migration of the idea, its repetition, its transformation. Elsewhere, he reiterated that Pushkin did not write separate pieces; rather they separated themselves as work progressed. You have not so much a ready idea awaiting verbal embodiment as a process in search of a constructive unity.[18] Creative history is not a simple rhetorical sequence: not the classical *inventio, dispositio, eloquentio.* Nor can it be reduced to the progression: conception, development and completion. Tomashevsky called for a study that would really take as its object Pushkin's work and not its individual parts.[19] Meylakh, too, lamented the fact that most essays about Pushkin dealt with separate works and thus could not furnish an integrated picture of Pushkin's artistic universe where many conceptions coexist or are interwoven in a complex, even contradictory way.[20] The Cleopatra text, since it never found its complete expression, more obviously hovers on the fluid boundaries where works diverge and converge in Pushkin's larger oeuvre. We have all the more reason to refer it to the whole.

There is an inherent value in establishing the cohesiveness of a great writer's imagination in all of its manifestations. However, the history of the Cleopatra cycle also has a bearing on such concrete literary-historical problems as the mutual adaptation of themes with genres and the succession of several different such adaptations, the stylistic orientation of the author—"romantic" yet "realistic"—and finally the definition of what is meant by "late Pushkin." The history of the Cleopatra text first shows us Pushkin as poet of the private self, then Pushkin in his public persona, and finally a Pushkin in whom the private and public selves coexist behind an aesthetic mask. The cycle embodies romantic poetry and realistic prose, but finally comes to express Pushkin's unique amalgam, the poetry of reality—and the reality of poetry.

But none of this would be especially gripping were it not for the moral pathos which emanates from the story at all of its stages. The cycle returns us again and again to the fateful moment held suspended in the Cleopatra poem from the beginning, a moment whose resolution is deferred by a striking clash of values. That will be the subject of the first chapter. Perhaps the poem's life and death question, more than anything, has sustained the efforts of several generations to penetrate the riddle of "Egyptian Nights."

I

BEGINNINGS: "CLEOPATRA"

The long story begins in 1824 with the poem, "Cleopatra."
Insofar as it is possible to paraphrase any lyric, the poem presents
Cleopatra presiding over a feast where she has fallen into a reverie.
From this reverie she rouses herself in order to issue a challenge by
which she offers a night of her love to any man who will agree to
forfeit his life on the morning after. Amid the general consternation
of the guests, three accept Cleopatra's terms. Cleopatra swears a
solemn oath to fulfill her bargain, and the lots of the three lovers are
drawn from an urn one by one. First comes the soldier, Aquila, then
the pleasure-seeker Crito, and last an anonymous youth on whom
Cleopatra fixes her gaze in admiration. On this the poem closes.

Cleopatra

The queen with voice and glance
Animated her luxurious feast,
All, praising Cleopatra in chorus,
Saw in her their idol,
They streamed noisily to her throne,
But suddenly over her golden cup
She fell into a reverie—and down
Drooped that wondrous head.

And the luxurious feast seems to drowse,
All is still in expectation...
But again she lifts her brow
And says with solemn mien:
"Attend me: I can restore
Equality between us.
Is there bliss for you in my love,
You can buy bliss:
Who will step up and bargain for passion?
I sell my nights.
Say, who among you will buy
A night of mine at the cost of his life?"

11

She had spoken. The crowd stood silent,
Every heart in agitation.
But Cleopatra waited,
Cold defiance on her face.
"I wait," she spoke, "so why this silence?
Now are you going to run away?
You were so many; step up,
Bargain for your night of joy."

And she cast a proud glance
Round her admirers...
Suddenly—one comes forth from their ranks,
After him two others.
Their step is bold, their eyes are bright.
The queen proudly rises.
It is accomplished: three nights are bought...
And the couch of death calls them.

Once again the queen has raised her proud voice:
"Forgotten today my crown and purple!
Like a simple concubine I mount the couch;
I serve you, o Cyprian, as none before,
A new gift to you is the prize of my nights.
O fearsome gods, hear then, gods of Hades,
Sad rulers of the terrors below!
Accept my vow: till the sweet dawn
Shall I obediently quench with the full chalice of love,
With wondrous soft pleasures and all the mysteries of the kiss
The last desires of them that possess me...
But no sooner shall Aurora's ray
Flash through the curtains into my chamber—I swear by my royal
    robes,—
Than their heads shall fall beneath the sword of morning!"

Blessed by consecrated hand,
The lots emerge from the urn one by one,
The first Aquila, bold follower of Pompey,
Scarred in battle, grown gray in the field.
He could not bear the woman's cold scorn
And stepped forth proudly, war's fierce son,
At the call of the last fateful pleasures,
As formerly he marched out to the glorious cry of battle.
Crito after him, Crito, the pampered sage,
    Reared beneath Argive skies
From his first days the follower and singer

Of ardent feasts and ardent Venus.
The last did not leave his name to the ages,
Known to none, famed for nothing;
A youth's down barely shadowed
    His modest cheek.
    The fire of love burned in his eyes,
    Love was written in his every feature—
He breathed Cleopatra, it seemed,
And the queen admired him long in silence.

(II, 222-24)

It is worth pausing over the nature and meaning of "Cleopatra" since whatever else "Egyptian Nights" will become by the end of Pushkin's life, the poem remains its core. In a revised form it is incorporated whole into the 1835 story, as an improvisation whose function it is to "model" the action of the implied plot—a projected repetition of the love drama which the improvisation serves actively to initiate. An alternative title for "Egyptian Nights" was still "Cleopatra" (J. VIII$_2$, 839). This is not to say that the later frame for the poem does not contribute themes of equal weight; it most certainly does. However, the poem's original context, the poetic universe which formed it yet against which it still stands out as unique, can also be conceived as the first frame for "Cleopatra." The original frame does not directly correspond with any later, deliberately constructed one, but it orients us through the genre coordinates of the poem—elegy, ballad, satire, and dramatic monologue—to the potential already latent in it. The original milieu of "Cleopatra" does not explain the genesis of the poem, for a poet's inspiration cannot be explained; rather, it shows what form the inspiration can take and where its general significance lies. Above all, the psychological foundation of the poem is more readily accessible on its first appearance in 1824.

Tomashevsky believed that "Cleopatra" was not connected with Pushkin's other conceptions and occupied a place apart in his work.[1] He reluctantly concluded that it was impossible to decide whether the idea for "Cleopatra" occurred to Pushkin in response to a stimulus from the outside or whether personal, lyric emotions found their expression in its plot.[2] But surely these terms are not mutually exclusive. Tomashevsky has simply formulated the essential problem: finding what is Pushkin's in the artistic make-up of "Cleopatra" and assessing his stake in the poem.

13

The basis for "Cleopatra" was an anecdote by Aurelius Victor about Cleopatra and her lovers, as Pushkin noted in the margin of the manuscript. Pushkin was reading him along with Tacitus and other ancient historians while preparing the theme of great men of past ages for his *Boris Godunov*. Here we have it, the external stimulus. Aurelius Victor provided a vehicle, but his anecdote does not account for the poem "Cleopatra." Even anecdote is too strong a term. Pushkin was struck by one line only which has absolutely no poetic realization in *De Viris Illustribus*. That is, in the Latin "source" there is no feast, no speech, no challenge, no oath, no cast of lovers, no significant breaking-off point. Aurelius Victor speaks only of Cleopatra's passion and of her nights which "many" obtained at the price of their lives. Pushkin refers to this one line in the fragment "Evening at the Dacha" (1835): "*Haec tantae libidinis fuit, ut saepe prostiterit: tantae pulchritudinis ut multi noctem illius morte emirent*" ("This woman was so lustful she often offered herself as a prostitute, so beautiful that many bought one of her nights with death").[3] In the source, this sentence is a mere aside in a collection of brief notes on the lives of Caesar, Mark Antony and Cleopatra—the famous lovers' triangle in which Pushkin shows no interest at all. Tomashevsky wrote that Pushkin "introduced into Aurelius Victor *only that* which turned historical information into an artistic picture" (emphasis added).[4] It is precisely Pushkin's artistic conception which made all the difference and which this chapter will take as its subject, discussing first the context and nature of the poem and then the central problem of its interpretation.

In the fall of 1824, when "Cleopatra" was being written, Pushkin was at Mikhaylovskoe, having left his southern exile behind him but not the "southern poems" or memories of southern loves. He entered the new poem into the black notebook embossed with Masonic symbols that he had brought back with him from Odessa. The draft breaks off after the description of the first lover; the second and third appear, one by one, separated by other material. The whole was transcribed as a fragment, a suggestive but self-contained psychological moment, into a clean notebook. In the same month of October, 1824, the Masonic notebook was filled variously with drafts of the *skazka*, "The Bridegroom," the end of a letter to Vyazemsky, "What is friendship, the slight flush of wine," "I am a king, but in chains," fragments from Chapter V of *Onegin*, and drafts for the "Imitations of the Koran" ("Arise, coward," "Not in vain did I dream of you"). Pushkin had just finished Chapter III of *Onegin*, put the final touches on *Gypsies* and written his "Second Epistle to the Censor."[5] In this sequence, we are often dealing not just with months (Mikhaylovskoe, autumn, 1824), but with a matter of days. Such is the original context.

"Cleopatra" 1824: Its Genre Universe

A convenient first approach to the nature of Pushkin's "Cleopatra" is to inquire about its genre. Genre, of course, means kind. Literary genres persisted for Pushkin not as rigid categories but rather as fluid expressive possibilities. What kind of poem did he make of this rather sensational material? First and foremost, "Cleopatra" was cast as historical elegy, the meter modulating in the accustomed meditative way from iambic tetrameter to Alexandrines. It was historical by setting and derivation, more legendary than factual, but springing out of the same historical readings which nourished *Boris Godunov*. It was elegiac in mood with the exasperated longings of its heroine-queen, the prospect of doomed love and the surge of emotion at the end for the nameless and inexperienced youth who offers himself up.

Perhaps it seems strange to call a poem in the third person like "Cleopatra" an elegy at all. Although it is not lyrical confession—it portrays "another"—this really means that it is elegy in an objective mode. It begins with a heroine who falls into the interesting and characteristic mood of melancholy: we have Cleopatra's situation of sorrow amidst the feast, her drooping head, the musings which bring on a speech that replaces the internal monologue of an elegy presented in the first person. But melancholy is a very incomplete criterion for elegy, which was the most advanced lyric form of its day. Though Pushkin takes a classical subject he deliberately casts it in the modern genre, elegy.[6] The elegy presents mixed feeling, which defines its historical role. In the elegy the complexity and differentiation of the inner life is disclosed along with the ceaseless ebb and flow of the psychological process. Thus, Cleopatra's modulation from animation to melancholy, back again to indignation and then to rapt admiration, forms the main charm of Pushkin's poem. An integral part of the new emotional formula of the elegy was often a brightening at the end, no matter how faint, a glimpse of something made perhaps more poignant by its unattainability. "Cleopatra" closes on just such a suggestion of spiritual renewal.

15

Each major poet who developed the elegy inclined by temperament and philosophy to seek for a different principle amidst the flux of the psychological process—be it a wavering metaphysical soul or a more concrete character with its conflicting dialectical movements and their story. In either case, the love elegy, the most advanced and popular of elegies, tended to acquire a larger dimension, philosophical or socio-historical. This mixture and the loss of equilibrium in the inner life—genre marks of the elegy—could ultimately be seen as equivalent to the stigmata of the modern hero. The conjunction of the personal with the historical or philosophical, or, in literary terms, of the lyric with the larger narrative or meditative forms, was the order of the day. Indeed, elegy naturally spills over into larger forms as it is realized that "mixedness" need not attach exclusively to the now-traditional elegiac states—melancholy, disillusion, and so on—and also that the clash of the various feelings within one character logically widens into the depiction of a conflict involving several such characters with their different psychological profiles. Thus, Pushkin's presentation of "Cleopatra" as historical elegy already implies its later develement directed toward finding the lines of intersection between history proper and elegy (the 1835 version of the poem). Thus, also, the affinity of the Cleopatra material with narrative: first with the "southern poems" which preceded it, and later with the society tale.

"Cleopatra" emerges from the sphere of the "southern poems," the harem of Bakhchisaray, the South of gypsy passion and also of Russian classical associations. The "southern poems" often transfer situations from elegies into narrative, as *The Prisoner of the Caucasus* does for "The orb of day has set" or *The Fountain of Bakhchisaray* for "The Tauride."[7] So it is possible to imagine Cleopatra as the heroine of a "southern poem" and conversely to conceive of "Cleopatra" as a kind of reduction of the romantic narrative, as perhaps one product of the disintegration of that genre.

It was in 1824 that Pushkin had published his "Excerpt from a Letter to D.," fragments touching his journey in the "Tauride," going back to Crimean impressions of 1820. Here he muses on why memory is fonder than experience, why he looks back now toward the ancient shore when he was so often unmoved while there or loved only a cypress or the sound of the sea. Yet the Temple of Diana and the ruins of Bakhchisaray made an impression: "Evidently, mythological legends are more fortunate for me than historical reminiscences" (VI, 634). The largely decorative use of historical reference in the

"Cleopatra" of 1824 does not make it merely an empty or neutral element in the scheme of the work which awaits concrete historical content. Rather, it signals the subject's real status as one of those legends having "mythological" imaginative presence.

The genealogy of Pushkin's Cleopatra stretches back to *The Fountain of Bakhchisaray* followed by *Gypsies* and forward to the plans for what later became "Egyptian Nights": Zarema/Zemfira—Zélie/Zinaida Volskaya. In the last development of Cleopatra's poem (1835), scenes of a harem re-emerge from this buried layer. *The Fountain of Bakhchisaray*, written in 1821-23, was published in 1824, and the poem "To the Fountain of Bakhchisaray Palace," also of 1824, testifies to Pushkin's vivid recollection of his southern poem. Compare Cleopatra with Girey in the opening of *The Fountain of Bakhchisaray*:[8]

Cleopatra:

> But suddenly over her golden cup
> She fell into a reverie—and down
> Drooped that wondrous head.
> And the luxurious feast seems to drowse,
> All is still in expectation . . .
> But again she lifts her brow
> And says with solemn mien . . .

Girey:

> Girey sat with lowered gaze;
> The amber pipe smoked in his lips;
> Silently an obsequious court
> Pressed round the dread khan.
> All was still in the palace;
> In awe all read
> The signs of anger and sorrow
> On his dark face . . .

> That severe brow
> Expressed more keenly the heart's agitation . . .

> What moves the proud soul?
> What thought possesses him?

(IV, 177)

17

The creation of *Gypsies* falls entirely within 1824. A reading of Pushkin's notes to the narrative shows his interest, simultaneously, in two aspects of the background: in the origin of the gypsies on the one hand—which, he protests, has nothing to do with the time-honored poetic etymology "gypsy/Egyptian"—and in the classical associations of the Russian South on the other. "Cleopatra" came to Pushkin between the writing of the tragic, second half of *Gypsies* and the final addition of its stark epilogue[9] whose words might define the keynote of "Cleopatra" as well: "*I vsiudu strasti rokovye, i ot sud'by zashchity net*" ("Everywhere the deadly passions reign, and there is no defense against the fates"). This stands in contrast to the suggestion of renewal offered by the end of the elegy "Cleopatra."

In the sequence of the Masonic notebook, "Cleopatra" appears out of the disintegration of *Gypsies* side by side with the "Imitations of the Koran," Pushkin's unorthodox poetic credo. In its original milieu, "Cleopatra" lay between Pushkin's southern manner and the eastern stylistic coloration of the "Imitations." The poet heaps ridicule on the unbelievers who did not rise to their mission: "derision to the faint-of-heart, they did not answer the call of war, putting no faith in the marvelous visions." Much as Cleopatra taunts her guests, Allah chides his prophet: "Arise, coward!" (II, 211). Devotion takes a fanatical and fatal hold in both cases. On the margin beside the text to the "Imitations of the Koran" Pushkin sketched a Mussulman raising his curving sword. Cleopatra concludes her solemn oath, which recalls the impressive series "I swear" intoned by the god of Islam at the beginning of the first "Imitation," with the promise: "Their heads shall fall beneath the sword of morning."[10]

In the autumn months of 1824 at Mikhaylovskoe Pushkin lived by his memories of the South. This means that "Cleopatra" belongs to Pushkin's love poetry. In 1825, reminiscences of Odessa surfaced in stanzas for "Onegin's Journey" in which Pushkin evoked a woman who resembles the languishing Cleopatra:

> And the box where, in brilliant beauty,
> A young merchant's wife,
> Haughty and languorous,
> Is surrounded by a crowd of slaves?
> She hears and doesn't hear
> The cavatina and their moans,
> And the joke mixed with flattery...
> While her husband—nods in the corner behind her...

(V, 208)

In 1826, a similar woman appears, now as a shade:

> You are no more, you to whom
> In the storms of my young life
> I am indebted for terrible experience
> And a sensual moment of paradise.

(V, 538, Ch. VI, variants)

However, in 1824, "Cleopatra" is most intimately related to one poem, the ballad "Persephone."[11] Cleopatra reveals the same face of love, or mask of love's goddess, as Pushkin's adaptation of the only disturbing scene from Parny's "Les Déguisements de Vénus."

Persephone

> The waves of Phlegethon plash,
> The vaults of Tartarus shake:
> The steeds of pale Pluto
> Rush the god from Hades
> Quickly to the nymphs of Pelion.
> Along the deserted shore
> Persephone follows,
> Indifferent and jealous,
> She takes the same road.
> *Timidly a youth bends*
> *His knee before the goddess.*
> Goddesses, too, find adultery tempting:
> *Persephone favors the mortal.*
> *The proud queen of hell*
> *Calls the youth with a glance,*
> She has clasped him and the chariot
> Already bears them to Hades:
> They fly, enveloped in a cloud;
> See the eternal meadows,
> Elysium and the somnolent banks
> Of languid Lethe.
> *There is immortality, there is oblivion,*
> *There are pleasures without end.*
> *Persephone enraptured,*
> *Without the purple or the crown,*
> *Submits to his desires,*
> *Yields to his kisses*
> *Her hidden beauties,*
> *Sinks in voluptuous pleasure,*

19

Silent, then languidly moaning...
But the hours of love fly past;
The waves of Phlegethon plash,
The vaults of Tartarus shake:
The steeds of pale Pluto
Quickly rush him back.
And Ceres' daughter departs
And leads the fortunate one after her
Out of Elysium
By a secret path;
Fortunate, he unlocks
With cautious hand
The door from whence stream
The false swarm of dreams.

(II, 179-80, emphasis added)

Cleopatra could be described as an elegy heroine involved in this ballad subject. The elegy gave scope for sophisticated analytic psychology, the ballad for archetypal, depth psychology. The combination was both rich and potent. "Persephone" is an erotic ballad which happens to be constructed around classical myth: the queen, herself abducted by the king of the underworld, allures a youth on a ride to Hades to share her bed, only to release him in the morning to return to earth through the gate of false dreams. We recognize the ballad ride, the ballad blending of love, hell and death, the ballad break of morn. Unlike "Cleopatra," "Persephone" has an ending and one with a twist: the youth lives to remember Elysium of the false dreams.

Both the "Persephone" ballad and "Cleopatra" are encompassed by a larger ballad complex in Pushkin which might be called "the bridegroom," after the poem "Zhenikh." The three lovers who present themselves for their night with Cleopatra are bridegrooms of sorts. "The Bridegroom" was in progress in 1824, with a draft coming in general terms not long after "Persephone" and "Cleopatra" in December of that year. Lines about Crito, Cleopatra's second lover, are actually intermingled with the drafts of "The Bridegroom."[12] The poem features a wedding feast that masks a trial climaxing in the execution of an impostor bridegroom: "Call the bridegroom to the feast... / And call the judge to the feasting" (IV, 414). Natasha's melancholy at the wedding feast brings us to the point where "Cleopatra" began:

20

Here is the bridegroom—all sit down,
    The glasses ring and thunder,
A health goes round;
    It's noisy, the guests are drunk.

Bridegroom

"Why, dear friends,
Does my beauteous bride
    Not eat, not drink, not serve us:
Why does the bride pine?"

(IV, 414)

The judgment of death against the bridegroom avenges his murder of an innocent girl (this is the robber bridegroom of folklore). Natasha refuses to be the next victim, becoming instead a heroine. Cleopatra's oath sworn by the gods of hell is also a judgment against men, remedy against their false, earthly oaths. The reckoning in "Cleopatra" follows different lines—it is the "price" of bliss—but the poem shares something of the moral atmosphere of retribution inherent in the bridegroom ballad. Cleopatra serves Venus—and Nemesis.

Nemesis against what? Against men, of course, but also against the pettiness of the world and the routine of society. As Cleopatra taunts her guests, ballad shades off into satire. Cleopatra swears by the gods of Hades not only because hell is the world of the dead and an underworld of hidden, black passions. Hell is also the "objective correlative" of society (*le monde*). As Akhmatova put it, "high society is a branch of hell."[13] This is the realm of Pushkin's *svetchern'*, the high and the brilliant as the base and black. Pushkin treats the society theme outright in a series of fragments which take Faust to hell, to the familiar banks of Phlegethon (1825). "What order and silence! / What an enormous procession of vaults..." All society is there: "Tell me, will the guests soon arrive?" (II, 306). Hell, as Persephone reminds us, belongs to Pluto, the god of wealth and the son of fortune. Cleopatra brazenly dares a mercenary society to be consistent about love: "Bargain for your night of joy." Dostoevsky spoke of her store of irony. But in 1824 social reference is still latent, outweighed by the primary imaginative presence. Historical prototypes, too, make themselves felt largely to cast a poetic aureole over Cleopatra.

21

Cleopatra is one of the great testers of men. In this she compares with Napoleon, the "man of fate." In her own way, she, too, confers a "fatal good fortune." Both control the mob, even to the point of enslaving their followers. Though Napoleon is tainted as hero, he is still the man who moved men and carried the fates with him for a time. Once he seemed to offer freedom, to cast a challenge in the face of reaction. The outline of the poem "The Watchman Drowsed Motionless on the Tsar's Doorstep" (1824), in which Napoleon confronts the court of Alexander I, presents a pattern of motifs similar to the composition of the Cleopatra poem. Compare: the drowsing watchman, the ruler and the lots, the palace, "it is accomplished," a sudden guest.

> The watchman drowsed motionless on the tsar's doorstep,
> The ruler of the North alone in his palace
> Sat silently wakeful, and the destinies of the world
> Lay compassed in that crowned head,
>> They fell by turn
> And brought the world the gift of peaceful servitude,—
> . . . .
> "It is accomplished!"—he spoke. . . .
>> The stroke of midnight sounds—
> And lo, a sudden guest appears in the tsar's palace.

(II, 175-76; 1824)

Cleopatra is a match for a hero like Napoleon. In "Evening at the Dacha," the penultimate stage in the Cleopatra cycle, Cleopatra vies with Napoleon's candidate for the title of foremost woman of the world, and by implication with Napoleon himself. Cleopatra dares a pampered court to break out of inertia, at the cost of their lives. She offers to restore equality, but promises that morning will bring the blade of execution.

Somewhere in the wings of the Cleopatra poem, beside Napoleon, there may stand the figure of Catherine the Great. Her magnificent journey down the Volga to the Crimea with her favorite and lover, Potemkin, in its time had elicited comparisons with Cleopatra and her fabled barque. De Ligne wrote ironically, "The Kievan Cleopatra does not swallow pearls, but distributes them in quantity."[14] In Pushkin's early historical notes, Catherine was a consummate hypocrite, a "Tartuffe in skirts," whose reign had corrupted Russian society and the Russian aristocracy, a woman for whom even dissipation was an arm of tyranny and lust a tool of power (VII, 127). The somewhat light-hearted verse equivalent from 1824 reads:

> Alas for that great woman,
> The woman who loved
> All forms of fame: the smoke of war
> And the incense of Parnassus.
>
> . . . .
>
> The dear old lady lived
> Pleasantly and a little loosely...

(II, 231)

Elegy, erotic ballad and satire do not exhaust the range of Pushkin's 1824 fragment. "Cleopatra" is also a theatrical poem. The declamatory passion, the fine rhetoric of the oath sworn by all the gods of Hades—all this is sustained with the intensity of classical tragedy. (The theatrical setting clings to Cleopatra to re-emerge in the device of the improvisation in "Egyptian Nights," where the heroine's speech is heard in a dramatic performance.) Pushkin was a devoted theatergoer in the period when he left the Lyceum and entered society. As Leonid Grossman put it in his *Pushkin at the Theater*, "The theatrical made powerful inroads on the love-life of the day."[15] The "Bohemian" theatrical life fostered a spirit of play with love; *teatral'nost'* ("the theatrical") was definitely an erotic element. However, the theater as a milieu did not overshadow Pushkin's interest in the theatrical repertoire, in the plays staged and the dramatic art which realized them. By descent Pushkin's Cleopatra may well be a heroine of the drama. When "Cleopatra" was done and Pushkin sat down to revise *Onegin*, he made room in Chapter I, in the theater scene, for a digression and a lament "Enchanted land... My goddesses, where are you?" It comes just as Onegin makes his entrance:

> Onegin flew to the theater,
> Where each, breathing the spirit of freedom
> Was ready to clap for an *entrechat*,
> Hiss Phèdre, Cleopatra...
>
> (*E.O.*, I, 17)

Here, Cleopatra, like Phèdre, figures as an eponym; she is a familiar theater name. As such, she recalls the heroines of Corneille's

Pompée and even Marmontel's notoriously bad *Cléopâtre*.[16] If Pushkin called to mind any Russian actress in the role of Cleopatra, it would surely have been Semyonova, admired for her Greek classic beauty, and the passionate flashes which illuminated her acting. Though Pushkin must have known *Antony and Cleopatra* and was even then planning his own Russian Shakespearean drama, *Boris Godunov*, in the evolution of "Cleopatra" Shakespeare comes later. The deepest layer for Pushkin's Cleopatra is laid down in material like Racine's, "the singer of kings and women in love,"[17] in the language of the passions (with just the beginning of concessions to softer *feelings* in the portrait of the youth and Cleopatra's admiration for him). We also seem to hear an aria from *opera seria*: which will it be, *vendetta* or *pietà*?

It is interesting that Cleopatra should be paired with Phèdre. The classic tragedy was played out under the empire of the passions and the fates. In each of the three works which take a decisive turn for Pushkin in 1824, the crux is the arrival of a moment of fate. Such moments transcend genre. In *Gypsies*: "Everywhere the deadly passions reign and there is no defense against the fates." In *Onegin*, when Tatyana falls in love: "It is decided in a higher place, it is heaven's will, I am yours." And then Cleopatra looms up before her dumbfounded court to offer herself, the knowledge of love and finally death to any taker. The poem proclaims, "it is accomplished" and the lots are cast, whether for certain doom or for ultimate deliverance still hangs in the balance. Meditative, passionate, indignant, dramatic, Cleopatra is the mistress of destiny.

"Cleopatra" 1824 and "Cleopatra" 1828

All these elements, then, can be said to enter into the spirit in which "Cleopatra" was conceived in 1824. The poem reappeared in 1828, when Pushkin revised it. This is the version which the editors of "Egyptian Nights" incorporated into the text of the story as its climax and conclusion. As we prepare to interpret the poem it will serve us to compare the new text with the old, reserving the question of its new context for later.[18]

> The palace shone. Singers thundered in chorus
> To the sound of flute and lyre.
> The queen with voice and glance
> Animated her luxurious feast;

All hearts swept toward her throne,
But suddenly over the golden cup
She fell into a reverie and down
Drooped that wondrous head...

And the luxurious feast seems to drowse,
The guests are silent, the chorus dumb.
But again she lifts her brow
And says with calm mien:
Is there bliss for you in my love?
You can buy bliss...
Attend me: I can restore
Equality between us.
Who will step up and bargain for passion?
I sell my love;
Say, who among you will buy
A night of mine at the cost of his life?—

—I swear...o mother of pleasures,
I shall serve you as none before,
Like a simple concubine I mount
The couch of passionate seduction.
Hear me, mighty Cyprian,
And you, infernal gods,
O gods of dread Hades,
I swear—until the dawn
I shall weary voluptuously
The desires of them that possess me
And quench them with wondrous soft pleasures
And all the mysteries of the kiss.
But no sooner shall immortal Aurora
Flash her morning purple,
I swear—beneath the fatal sword
Shall fall the heads of those fortunate ones.

She has spoken—horror seizes them all,
And they shudder with passion...
She hears their confused murmur
With cold defiant face,
And she casts a scornful glance
Round her admirers...
Suddenly one emerges from the crowd,
After him two others.
Their step is bold; their eyes are bright;
She rises to meet them;

It is accomplished; three nights are bought,
And the couch of death calls them.

    Blessed by the priests,
From the fatal urn
Before the motionless guests
Now fall the lots one by one.
The first—Flavius, the bold warrior,
Grown gray in the Roman legions;
He could not bear the woman's
Haughty scorn;
He accepted the challenge of pleasure
As once in days of war
The call of fierce battle.
After him Crito, the young sage,
Born in the groves of Epicurus,
Crito, the follower and singer
Of the Graces, Venus and Cupid...
Fair to heart and eye,
Like a spring flower barely opened,
The last did not leave
His name to the ages. The first down
Tenderly shadowed his cheek;
Rapture shone in his eyes:
The inexperienced force of passion
Burned in his young heart...
And with softened feeling
The queen rested her gaze upon him.

(VI, 386-89)

In general outline the original poem had read: Cleopatra's feast, her challenge, repetition of the challenge with a taunt (rhetorically—intensification and amplification), acceptance, Cleopatra's oath, and the drawing of the lots which included the presentation of the three lovers. In 1828 it reads: feast, challenge, oath, acceptance, and drawing of lots. The repetition is eliminated and the oath becomes the second wave of Cleopatra's speech. The moment of suspense and choice is postponed until just before the end. The result is a more unified dramatic movement instead of the stiffer symmetry of two psychological moments. The oath is the pivot upon which the composition turns. It also had the closest connections with "Persephone" of 1824. Now they are partly masked. The poem's metrical identification with the elegy and with the classical

26

declamatory mode—the original Alexandrines which contrasted with the introductory four-foot iambic and the occasional five-foot lines toward the end—is also lost as they are absorbed into a single meter, in about as many lines. (Bryusov was astonished by this feat of virtuosity.[19])

Pushkin is also able to enrich by stylistic means the poem whose composition he condensed. Through a kind of sophisticated chemistry, nouns are changed to epithets, epithets to nouns, epithets find new attachments, and a few telling ones make their appearance. In the process, Pushkin sharpens the contrast in tone which has fueled a controversy over his Cleopatra. In the first place, the entire layer of elegiac-sentimental vocabulary is moderated and largely replaced by a more severe and impersonal diction. It is *sladostrastnyi* for *sladostnyi*; Venus is dignified under the name *mater' naslazhdenii*, and the couch is *lozhe strastnykh iskushenii*. The *bogi ada, podzemnykh uzhasov pechal'nye tsari* are reduced to *podzemnye tsari*, and the rather conventional "cup of love" is absorbed into the verb *utoliu*. Cleopatra's curtained chamber is gone; Pushkin rejects the appurtenances of the intimate boudoir which might detract from the climax of the oath. Toward the end comes the most striking shift: the "ray of dawn" (*Avrory luch*), originally a mythological cue for the final drama and then a figure of anticipation for the executioner's flashing axe, has grown into the immortal goddess of the dawn in person, *Avrora vechnaia*. The robes of porphyry which had belonged to Cleopatra—*klianus' moei porfiroi*—become the raiment of the dawn. Cleopatra retires behind the inexorable figure of light who is no longer merely an accessory and herald. The former "sword of morning" has now become openly thematic. The section closes with a new irony: "I swear, beneath the fatal sword shall fall the heads of those fortunate ones." Cleopatra still swears by the goddess of love—now *moshchnaia Kiprida*—and by the powers of hell; and each is still given equal weight. But they are now more powerful than they are compassionate. The gods of hell are not "sad." But the reckoning does not come from out of the dark underworld. It comes more clearly now through the agency of the powers of light. At the end Cleopatra becomes almost a bystander.

Through the 1828 poem, Pushkin takes a second measure of Cleopatra's character. She has kept her "cold defiance," and now her face is scornful as well as proud. If the challenge had agitated her guests before, now horror grips them and their hearts shudder with passion. Yet Cleopatra's character is not so much lowered as it is strengthened. Her impatient and undignified second taunt to the

27

assembled guests is eliminated. And she is once again not entirely possessed by a single ruthless passion as "classic" characters were, according to Pushkin.[20] She has a divided or "romantic" nature. She still bows her wondrous head in the midst of the feast: *ponikla divnoiu glavoi. Divnaia nega* and *tainy lobzan'ia* are permitted to stand as the elements of her love-potion. She confers *blazhenstvo*, perfect bliss. Most importantly, her final enigmatic expression is qualified from rapt admiration (*i molcha dolgo im tsarista liubovalas'*) to *umilenie*. She does not just look on the youth with wonder, marveling at his ardor as at a spectacle viewed from outside. Now her own heart is touched.

Of course, Cleopatra is not the sole focus of the poem. There are two centers, the queen and her lovers. These emerge from the throng of guests which is psychologically derived from the motif of the "passionate crowd," the *strastnaia tolpa* of Pushkin's "Can You Forgive Me My Jealous Fancies":

> Surrounded by a crowd of admirers,
> Why do you want to seem gracious to all,
> And why does your glance bestow on all an empty hope,
> Now tender, now melancholy?
> ....
> Do you not see it when, in their passionate crowd,
> Strange to conversation, alone and silent,
> I am tormented with lonely vexation...

> (II, 161; 1823)

They seek in love the "tyrannical dreams" or "imperious dreams" of Pushkin's "Women," meant for Chapter IV of *Onegin* (variants, J. VI, 538). These are no longer the three youths doing battle for the hand of the lovely princess, as in *Ruslan and Lyudmila*.[21] By 1828, the first, the graying warrior, is bold but no longer proud. War, like the love he seeks, has become fierce but not glorious (*slavnyi krik srazhenii* becomes *vyzov iarogo srazhen'ia*). The second candidate, Crito, still a poet-lover, is now identified as an Epicurean. *Mudrets*, wise man or sage, takes on a new quasi-philosophical overtone. The first two lovers embody the kindred attitudes *otvazhnost'* and *bezpechnost'*, respectively; the one lives for fame, the other for pleasure. The second lover is blander; the *fire* is reserved for the third, nameless youth. The tension set up in the grouping is reminiscent of the character models tested in Pushkin's early epistles: soldier, poet, impetuous youth. They are characteristically gathered at the poetic "feast" of life. The three lovers fit into quite separate poetic contexts: the first, into the old-fashioned amorous chivalry, Mars paying court to Venus; the second, into the amatory style cultivated in the new *poésie fugitive*; the third fits into no convention but the nature of youth and desire.

He is actually introduced with a simile, and a new one—contrary to the strict economy imposed on the rest of the poem. This signals a new climax. But the comparison itself is unusual; it falls just short of sentimentality; it is drawn in a deliberately naive vein: "Fair to heart and eye / Like a spring flower barely opened." This implicit appeal for mercy takes the place of the "modest cheeks," "fire of love" and "he breathed Cleopatra." But the sentiment is with the beholder. The youth himself is possessed by passion. "Rapture shone in his eyes, the inexperienced force of passion burned in his young heart..." Of "love" there is not a word. The middle ground has disappeared. The youth and Cleopatra develop as a study in contrary motion. When the two of them face each other in the end, there is nothing left but passion on the one side and pity on the other. Cleopatra's final expression cost Pushkin much thought, for it was particularly important: *pechal'nyi vzor, tomnyi vzor, vzor vnimatel'nyi, luch zhalosti* (J. III, 691-92). Sadness, longing, curiosity, love, pity and tenderness all contended for the spot. One might even say that the poem was written for the sake of its significant breaking-off point. The significance can better be appreciated in the wider context of Pushkin's work.

Umilenie

"Cleopatra" ends with an upsurge. These moments of feeling, these flashes, have always impressed readers of Pushkin. Gershenzon, in his *Pushkin's Wisdom*, dedicated a chapter to them entitled, significantly enough, "*Umilenie*."[22] Pushkin's demon experiences the moment in a poem called, of course, "The Angel":

The spirit of denial, the spirit of doubt
Looked upon the pure spirit
And felt for the first time, dimly,
The spontaneous warmth of tenderness [*umilenie*].
"Farewell,"—he spoke,—"I have seen you,
And you have not shone on me in vain:

I have not hated all in heaven,
I have not scorned all on earth."

(III, 17; 1827)

There is the awakening of "I remember a wondrous moment" and the
kindred one in the "Imitations of the Koran":

I remember a wondrous moment:
You appeared before me,
Like a fleeting vision,
Like the spirit of pure beauty.

. . . .

Years passed. Mutinous storm gusts
Dispersed my former dreams...

. . . .

My soul had an awakening:
And here you have again appeared,
like a fleeting vision,
Like the spirit of pure beauty.

And my heart beats in rapture,
As for it spring to life once more
Its god and inspiration,
And life and tears and love.

(II, 267; 1825)

The "Imitations" end with the wonder and amazement of the traveler
who has murmured against his god but awakens from a trance,
during which years have passed, to find refreshment, new faith and
youth restored:

And a miracle was performed then in the desert:
The past sprang to life again with new beauty...

. . . .

And the traveler feels both strength and joy;
Youth reborn leapt in his blood...

(II, 213; 1824)

30

Pushkin is periodically haunted by a psychological plot in which a character receives a vision of beauty and the good which impresses itself strongly upon him: the native girl reawakens a stirring of feeling and thus life in the disillusioned prisoner of the Caucasus, Maria in Girey, Tatyana in Onegin. Whether with the vision comes the strength to abide by it is another question. Thus, it may be that Cleopatra will nevertheless destroy the youth. Pushkin's central heroes, Onegin and quite possibly Don Juan, will be punished for believing in feeling too late. As Pushkin commented on the character of the "modern man" in *Onegin*, we all have our sights fixed on vanity and power... feeling to us is odd and laughable (*E.O.*, II, 14; 1823).

Tomashevsky stated the crucial problem of interpretation, therefore, when he contrasted the cruel logic of the poem "Cleopatra" popularized by the symbolists, with what he was convinced was the psychological paradox of compassion which Pushkin intended.[23] Bryusov's article of 1910 seems to leave some room for doubt as to the outcome of the Cleopatra plot:

> Pushkin did not complete his poem. He showed us what great temptation and what terrible power sensuality holds for the human being. He showed us how men are prepared to plunge into this black abyss even if they have to pay for it with their lives. He alluded to the mysterious closeness of passion and death. But Pushkin did not finish speaking the words he began to utter.
>
> What might have followed? Did Pushkin wish to present an image of the nights which had been bought? Three attitudes to passion and death of three different souls? And Cleopatra's attitude toward them? Perhaps in the verse that followed he wished to lend a somewhat more humane aspect to the image of Cleopatra, which remains in the completed part of the poem almost the soulless incarnation of beauty and temptation? Is not this what is suggested by the lines of the original version where Cleopatra cannot contain her feeling of grief on seeing the third of them who shall possess her?... There is no answer to our questions. Pushkin carried the mystery of his poem to the grave.[24]

But Bryusov's reading of "Cleopatra" made it possible for him to try to finish the fragment with scenes of the promised nights which inexorably take their appointed course. He actually found something to admire in the "soulless incarnation of beauty and temptation": Cleopatra, the "strong personality." As imperious and indifferent as the gods, she expressed for Bryusov the highest ideal of man that antiquity could offer. He was not a little nostalgic for its imagined "wholeness."[25]

Tomashevsky held that the poem "Cleopatra" was a deliberate fragment whose chief interest lay in its final psychological situation:

> The opinion exists that the poem remained unfinished. I will return later to the origin of this opinion, but direct aquaintance with the 1824 version gives no grounds to conclude that the elegy was unfinished. Pushkin would hardly have made a fair copy of a poem which had not been brought to completion. What is more, there are no attempts to sketch a continuation either in the fair copy or the draft. And in reality the psychological conflict of the poem consists in the fact that the brazen, cold challenge of Cleopatra is to some extent defeated by the love of the youth who has accepted it out of far different motives than the cold ones which governed the warrior who could not bear a woman's "cold scorn," and the sage, the pampered devotee of sensual pleasures. Cleopatra is all but won over by the youth's love. This is the concluding psychological situation of the elegy. And Pushkin, evidently, in no way intended to continue the elegy and describe Cleopatra's nights since such a continuation could not enrich the psychological characterization of Cleopatra.[26]

Where Bryusov saw the sinister erotic ballad as predominant, Tomashevsky saw the elegy. While for Bryusov Cleopatra easily becomes the incarnation of passion or the spirit of "antiquity," for Tomashevsky she never ceases to be a human portrait. The two readings differ largely in emphasis and were supported by two compositional solutions of an editorial problem. In revising the poem, Pushkin had placed a sign of transposition before Cleopatra's oath but neglected to indicate where the section should be moved. Zhukovsky, assuming that the poem implied a continuation, transferred the oath to the end. This was the version which impressed itself on nineteenth-century readers: even having seen her lovers, Cleopatra swears to destroy them. Tomashevsky, for whom the poem was a studied fragment, combined the oath with the rest of Cleopatra's previous speech, leaving the psychological paradox to resonate as the poem's final statement.[27]

Actually, all the terms of interpretation for "Cleopatra" were first formulated by Dostoevsky in 1861 and have remained constant: a mixture of attraction and repulsion balanced against a different sort of wonderment. Dostoevsky was convinced that the poem was complete in itself, though, of course, he knew it in its nineteenth-century version.

As Pushkin presented the subject, Dostoevsky begins, it was not titillating but shattering. Cleopatra represents a sated society, without faith, without thought, without aim, without future, for which all that is left is contained in the body and in the search for new and powerful sensations. After this historical prelude, which anticipates the poem's later development in Pushkin, Dostoevsky concentrates on a psychological portrait of Cleopatra at the crucial lyrical moment:

> But hers is a strong soul ... it has a store of strong and spiteful irony. Irony which has stirred in it now. The queen has conceived a desire to astound all these guests by her challenge; she wants to enjoy her contempt for them ... But the thought has already taken complete possession of her soul ... O, now she, too, would like them to accept her monstrous challenge! ... What demonic happiness to kiss her victim, to love it, to become its slave for a few hours, to quench its every desire with all the mysteries of the kiss ... and at the same time to know every minute that this victim, this momentary lord and master will pay with his life for this love and for the proud insolence of his momentary dominion over her ... Mad cruelty has long since warped this divine soul and often already reduced it to the likeness of a beast.... In her beautiful body is concealed the soul of a darkly fantastical horrible reptile; it is the soul of a spider who, they say, eats her mate at the moment of their union.... But the soul of the poet could not bear this picture; would not end it with Cleopatra the hyena, and for one instant he made her human ... for a moment the human being awakened and the queen looked with compassion on the youth. She could still feel compassion [*umilit'sia*]! ... But only for a moment ... You understand to what kind of people our Divine Redeemer then came.[28]

Dostoevsky's reading of the poem seems to lead back to the interpretation of "Egyptian Nights" offered by its first commentator, Annenkov. He saw the story as depending on the inherent clash of the classical anecdote with the modern sensibility.[29] The reader need not immediately make up his mind about the historical or religious underpinnings of such an interpretation, but he cannot escape recognizing the poignancy of Cleopatra's dividedness. The poem will not yield a single resolution, and its very ambiguity leaves the way open for further development.

Umilenie—the word is used of one aspect of the Orthodox iconography of the Virgin and Child and implies a world of sentiments quite outside the realm of Cleopatra, the devourer of men. In any case, passions are fatal, but feelings salutary; one way lies doom and the other the possibility of deliverance.

Yet there is also life in Cleopatra's fire by contrast with her dull court; death would be preferable to that mediocrity. Cleopatra's word—the challenge and oath—and her glance, have been the moving agents all along. "She drooped her wondrous head," now again she "raises her brow and says with calm mien," "she cast a scornful glance round her admirers." At the fateful moment her lovers' eyes are bright—and Cleopatra lets her glance rest. She does, in fact, animate her feast even while she swears that death will strike down her lovers. This principle of animation lies at the heart of the whole poem and has an important part to play in forming the later variations on the Cleopatra theme. The poem cannot be reduced to one logical conclusion, or even to a single psychological paradox. The tensions are too complex. A sweeping, oscillating movement follows Cleopatra as she lowers, then raises her head, as she at last rises from her seat to "ascend" the couch where she will lie down with her lovers. She sells her nights, calls on the gods of darkness, but finally evokes the dawn. She is by turns queen, common concubine, and queen again. We progress from a glimpse of the "last" moments and pleasures to contemplate the untried youth, for whom everything is beginning—and the poem comes to an end. It balances its contradictions.

* * *

The poem has also acquired a setting; the first two lines are new:[30] "The palace shone. Singers thundered in chorus to the sound of flute and lyre." The classical décor is thus concretely and physically established. But these two lines add more than a setting. The insistent presence of the guests and the chorus, of the audience, now punctuates the poem. ("Singers thundered in chorus . . . the guests are silent, the chorus dumb . . . she hears their confused murmur.") This presentation leads into the future development of the same themes in prose, in "Egyptian Nights," and more directly, it parallels Pushkin's first approaches to a similar story in 1828 in "The Guests Gathered at the Dacha."

The various components of the 1824 "Cleopatra" each had a future in the further unfolding of the material contained within it. From the psychological side of elegy sprang the study of character pursued in the society tale; from its historical side, the famous correspondences between "two worlds," ancient and modern. From the ballad came the "evenings" or "nights" atmosphere charged with sinister meaning, and also the magnetic impulse of animation in the figurative underworld, the "hell" of society. From the satirical aspect stemmed the various conversations about Russian society which appear in 1828/30. From the theatrical presentation came, at last, the device of poetic improvisation in "Egyptian Nights." The original Cleopatra staged her own scene and invented her own plot; she had a power of dramatic conception that made her the imaginative match for a poet.

Two fundamental questions are set for the Cleopatra cycle by the terms of the original poem: what is Cleopatra and who are her lovers? The first involves a more accurate estimation of Cleopatra's character, which must be perceived as a divided one. The second eventually leads to the fusion of the Cleopatra theme with the theme of the divided poet. At the same time the sentence of death that hangs over the head of Cleopatra's lovers comes to rest on the poet. Thus, "Egyptian Nights" at last absorbs the Cleopatra poem. But this occurs only at the end of a long development. In an early moment of retrospection, however, in September of 1824, Pushkin had already asked, what does life really amount to but one or two nights?—"*Vsia zhizn', odna li, dve li nochi?*" (II, 196). The Cleopatra poem puts the same question again. In the desperation of love there can be only one answer: yes, it all comes down to one or two nights. Society cares nothing for it; psychology, history and religion have nothing to do with it, the core experience is absolute.

II

POEM INTO PROSE: "THE GUESTS GATHERED AT THE DACHA" (1828)

The question now arises how Cleopatra came into prominence again in 1828, and how the second version of the poem emerged as one result. The chronology follows these lines: in July and August of 1828, Pushkin sang the impetuous Zakrevskaya ("The Portrait," "The Confidant"); in August and early September, he wrote "The Guests Gathered at the Dacha," the first frame for "Cleopatra," adding the section "Minsky still lay abed" in the latter part of October. He rewrote "Cleopatra," apparently, at the end of October or the beginning of November. In related spheres, the whole of *Poltava* was completed in October: the third canto was finished on the 19th, the dedication written on the 27th. Several important sections were added, however, in the first part of November. On November 4, Pushkin put the finishing touches on Chapter VII of *Onegin*, completing the fair copy of the entire chapter. About the same time, again in the first half of November, he wrote or revised such important poems as "The Upas-Tree," "The Poet and the Crowd," and "In the Sweet Shade of the Fountains."

Such is the context of the second "Cleopatra" in the creative process of 1828. Pushkin returned to the poem after working through variations on its themes in the Zakrevskaya cycle and in "Guests." Its particular fusion of elements still seems to have fulfilled artistic needs which other modes left unsatisfied. The contemporary voice, whether heard in the lyric or in prose, could not say it all. There is no evidence that the poem was intended in any way for "Guests." Poem and prose were still separate. Pushkin often modulated his material from genre to genre, as with the subject of "The Blackamoor of Peter the Great" which he tried in folk stylization, in the unfinished story (as historical fiction), and in the plan "I have often reflected on that terrible family story" (the plain domestic novel approach). In the story of the Cleopatra material, then, this chapter actually takes us back. The poem "Cleopatra" of 1828 was the end put to the first developments in prose, and not their herald.[1] It continued to live its own independent life.

37

The year 1828 marked the limit of a period. *Poltava* ended in a graveyard of memories, as Chapter VII of *Onegin* began in one, at Lensky's tomb. It was a year for rededications: now Pushkin introduced a new edition of *The Prisoner of the Caucasus*; he wrote the dedication to *Ruslan and Lyudmila* and also the material he later used as the dedication to *Onegin* as a whole. He now interjected the ironic invocation of the Muse at the end of Chapter VII. In 1828 the Cleopatra theme is also remembered and rededicated, that is, redirected.

This was also a year of crisis for Pushkin and his audience; the honeymoon was ending as he faced the problems of maturity, popularity and the fickle crowd. If popularity was a sore point in relations with the public, propriety was the nub with the government and Pushkin's several censors. 1828 was the year of the *Gavriliad* affair, as 1827 had been the year of the cause célèbre, "André Chénier." The more satisfying, then, to take up another provocative subject.

There was, of course, a psychological context as well as a strictly literary one. As Akhmatova put it, 1828 was Pushkin's "wildest year": "... the researcher is threatened with the danger of losing his way in the beautiful flower-bed of amours: when Olenina and Zakrevskaya coincide, when Pushkin boasts of his victory with Kern, when he undoubtedly is somehow linked with Khitrovo and when, at the same time, he was Mickiewicz's rival for Sobanskaya. And all this is in Petersburg alone."[2] Pushkin felt threatened again with disgrace and banishment ("Again Clouds Gather Over Me"), perhaps felt projected in spirit back to the years of exile in the South. In any event, 1828 saw new poems on the Crimea and Saadi, a backward glance at the experiences of *The Fountain of Bakhchisaray*, complicated by Pushkin's new friendship with Mickiewicz, author of *The Crimean Sonnets*. However, the overwhelming fact of Pushkin's situation from the middle of 1826 through 1828 was his restoration to society and the capital cities. Society included the companionship of poets like Mickiewicz, Baratynsky and Griboedov. These years were a time of dialogue with Germanophile philosophical-artistic youth in Moscow. Society, government and journalism formed the milieu of a new public life for the poet which proved consistently disappointing. Pushkin alternated between immersing himself in society and casting about for a way out—either to home and marriage or to travel and adventure. Marriage and travel being both denied him, the one by

Olenina's refusal, the other by Benkendorf's, Pushkin, in Vyazemsky's phrase, "whirled all summer in the vortex of society, [and] sang Zakrevskaya."[3] In his letters he made himself out to be *l'homme du monde*—as when he styled himself Lovelace writing to a friend Valmont (X, 252), or when he teased a middle-aged lady admirer with hints of a passionate liaison elsewhere (X, 251; to Khitrovo). He contributed his part to "the completely unbelievable love life and mutual relations between that day's youth of both sexes," as Modzalevsky expressed it.[4] So the upswing of an inner cycle in Pushkin's development found him in a changed ambiance before a changed audience. It was perhaps natural that this "wildest year" saw the revival of the Cleopatra theme. But Pushkin's new public role, his developing political and intellectual interests and, above all, the conflicting demands of society and self all acted to shape the old material in new ways. They contributed to produce the fragment "The Guests Gathered at the Dacha."

"Cleopatra" into Society Tale

Bondi doubted that "Guests" had any relation to the Cleopatra story as told in "Egyptian Nights."[5] But the filiation of "Guests" (1828) with the fragment "We Spent the Evening at the Dacha" (1835) is clear enough, and the close tie of "Evening at the Dacha" with "Egyptian Nights" is also evident. To exclude "Guests" would mean to break an extremely important link in the chain which leads from 1824, through 1828, to the story of 1835. In Pushkin's middle period, the Cleopatra material develops along the lines of biography and social criticism, acquiring a new depth and breadth, but at the expense of its original mythological imaginative presence. Pushkin proposes different answers to the questions of what Cleopatra is and who are her lovers, reorienting the characters. The center of the original poem was Cleopatra's dramatic monologue; in "Guests," two thematic dialogues provide a commentary to her situation as Pushkin tries to develop a "general conversation" to encompass the personal drama. The setting is exclusively contemporary life, the genre is society tale and the obligatory medium is prose.

Moreover, the traces of "Cleopatra" are not so deeply buried in "Guests." What we had in the poem was only an introduction to a projected action. In "Guests" the dramatic situation of "Cleopatra" remains, for the meantime stripped of its historical dress. The poem is actually submerged in the opening of the story whose lyrical aura signals that it is a condensed poetic reminiscence. The picture of the lighted palace resounding to music (lines 1-2) is paralleled by the spectacle of society gathering at a fashionable dacha after the Italian opera. These are the same "guests" even though the feast has been displaced by society occasions. The card tables do service for the motif of the lots. For the moment, an important conversation may be omitted from discussion. Here is the general picture as Volskaya arrives; it follows the poem quite faithfully:

> The guests gathered . . . Volskaya ascended the stairs . . . her large, black eyes, her liveliness of movement, the very eccentricity of her dress, all could not help but attract attention . . . but Volskaya noticed nothing . . . she gazed abstractedly in all directions; her face, changeable as a cloud, depicted vexation; she sat down . . . and, as they say, *se mit à bouder*. Suddenly she shuddered and turned round . . . She rose . . . The guests were leaving . . . Volskaya suddenly noticed the dawn . . . Minsky helped Volskaya into her carriage. "It is your turn, it seems," a young officer said to him. "Not at all," he answered, "she is otherwise engaged."

(VI, 560-63)

In the draft to "Guests," Volskaya was even closer to Cleopatra. She was at first more languid, and she preserved the characteristic motifs: "her appearance enlivened society" and "she fell into a reverie," "was lost in thought" (J. VIII$_2$, 544, 545). At the end of the first section of the fragment we overhear Volskaya and Minsky discuss the selection of lovers from whom Volskaya can choose. Thus, Volskaya is certainly related to Cleopatra. In the plans for an extended story she is called Zélie (Zeliya), "*une femme à la mode.*" There she is also contrasted with another woman, "*une jeune provinciale.*"

For in 1828 "Cleopatra" was to be drawn into a new frame of reference. This is expressed in the character alignments. In the original elegy Cleopatra's choice as lover is obviously the youth. In "Guests," it is his natural successor, the disillusioned "man of the world." It is as though the character had aged along with Pushkin's memories, as though Pushkin had decided, yes, such a hero is more her lover now. What then becomes of the original psychological paradox produced by the confrontation of Cleopatra and the youth? It has not been sacrificed, but displaced. All romance subjects lend themselves to twin heroines, demonic and angelic. The first example

40

in Pushkin is the pair Zarema and Maria in *The Fountain of Bakhchisaray*. In 1828, a figure like Volskaya enters into a wider plan in opposition to a rival. I refer to Pushkin's outline for a story to which the fragment "Guests" was to have been the introduction (VI, 788-89). Having discarded the youth as a possible hero, Pushkin supplies another naive character to confront the "Cleopatra" and to touch her heart, a young provincial girl. The youth has vanished. He belongs to a kindred but different plot. In the extended plan the hero Minsky is the one placed between a romantic and a sentimental love—Volskaya and the young girl. But only Volskaya stands to be in some way redeemed through her rival. Pushkin hesitates between their reconciliation and Zélie's unmitigated defeat by the provincial girl who in turn becomes the victim of society.

Matching heroine with hero, Pushkin clearly means Volskaya and Minsky for each other. The other lovers whom they discuss— who roughly parallel Cleopatra's original three—only serve to bring Volskaya under Minsky's sway. The two are paired for a reason. The second section of "Guests" shows how very nearly Pushkin imagined his new Cleopatra, Volskaya, in terms of the experience of the hero of his times. Her off-hand education and early introduction into society are like Onegin's. We are given pictures of the social round, her caprices. At first her childish frivolity is welcome; it breaks the staid monotony of aristocratic society. But when she fails to grow up, Volskaya becomes the object of malicious gossip, which she decides to justify by her rebellion. It goes without saying that Minsky is drawn to Volskaya by elective affinity, as she is to him. "Zinaida singled out Minsky; apparently a certain similarity of character and situation was to bring them together" (VI, 564). Minsky is the man of the world, cousin to Onegin and to Constant's Adolphe. He is also the familiar Don Juan. Pushkin removed from the draft the telltale cape (J. VIII$_2$, 537), but his appearance in association with the Spanish traveler remained to lend its aura. Minsky, too, was punished by slander for his loose morals and is in revolt against social convention. When Minsky and the Spaniard are transformed into Charsky and the Italian improvisor, when they become a pair of poets, it will still be well to remember that Charsky's predecessor was Volskaya's lover, and that they had a great deal in common (see Chapter IV). They sprang from the same root in Pushkin's imagination: "*l'homme du monde*," "*une femme à la mode*."

Obviously, Pushkin has recast "Cleopatra" as a society tale. This was a natural enough transformation in a social setting which enjoyed mythological salon charades as an elegant game. Anna Kern

41

recounts in her memoirs how, one evening, when she had drawn the role of Cleopatra, Pushkin paid her the compliment of a rather-too-forward witticism:

> As we continued to play, Cleopatra fell to my lot, and, when I was holding the basket of flowers, Pushkin along with my cousin, Alexander Poltoratsky, came up to me, looked at the basket and pointing to my cousin, said, "*Et c'est sans doute Monsieur qui fera l'aspic?*" I found this impertinent, made no answer and left.[6]

Here is Pushkin's plan for developing "Guests" into an extended society tale. Characteristically, it is mostly in French, the language of society:

> L'homme du monde fait la cour à une femme à la mode, il la séduit et en épouse une autre *po raschetu*. Sa femme lui fait des scènes. L'autre avoue tout à son mari. L'autre la console, la visite. L'homme du monde malheureux, ambitieux.
>
> L'entrée d'une jeune personne dans le monde.
>
> Zélie aime un égoiste vaniteux; entourée de la froide malveillance du monde; un mari raisonnable; un amant qui se moque d'elle. Une amie qui s'en éloigne. Devient légère, fait un esclandre avec un homme qu'elle n'aime pas. Son mari la répudie. Elle est tout à fait malheureuse. Son amant, son ami.
>
> 1) Une scène du grand monde at the dacha of Count L.—the room is crowded, about tea-time—the arrival of Zeliya—she turns her eyes to l'homme du monde and spends the entire evening with him.
> 2) background account de la séduction—la liaison, son amant l'affiche—
> 3) L'entrée dans le monde d'une jeune provinciale. Scène de jalousie, ressentiment du grand monde—
> 4) Bruit du mariage—désespoir de Zélie. Elle avoue tout à son mari. Son mari raisonnable. Visite de noces. Zélie tombe malade, réparait dans le monde; on lui fait la cour, etc., etc.

(VI, 788-89)

The adulation of Cleopatra's palace crowd translates as "*on fait la cour à une femme à la mode.*" The silent guests become "*la froide malveillance du monde.*" The protagonists of the existing fragments of "Guests" are shown against a picture of society at large. In

"Guests," the men form a frame around the women: "The ladies took their places on the sofas. A circle of men formed around them." In the draft, the tea-table from which the society hostess presided was another circle to be reckoned with. Then there are the card-tables. These are all charmed circles, the orbits of the social planetary system. They represent the order of things: "Order was established," "a circle formed," "the whist tables were organized." You took your turn for tea, tried your chance at cards. When the guests gather, they naturally assemble into these circles: *"gosti s"ezzhalis'."* But on a definite tangent to society we have Minsky and Volskaya: *"elle est singulière";* (J. VIII₂, 547), "this is unheard of," *"èto ni na chto ne pokhozhe."* The daring lovers are gone from the picture. There is only the sphere of "contemporary man"—*"l'homme du monde," "égoiste vaniteux," "l'homme du monde malheureux, ambitieux."* With the shift to the contemporary scene we sacrifice historical anecdote to *"istoricheskii rasskaz de la séduction."*[7] The frame of the story is much simpler than the future "Egyptian Nights." Cleopatra always had a past (as the thoughtful heroine of elegy), now she and Minsky each have a biography. To delve into the past of his heroine, to go back and show how she became a society "Cleopatra," Pushkin gives up the other past of historical projection. This is what happens in 1828.

It is easy to underestimate the importance of the society tale as a genre.[8] It enjoys none of the prestige of the historical novel in the eyes of Soviet critics who are perhaps influenced by the vulgarized and moralized travesties of the society tale current in Russia in the 1830's. But as Vyazemsky commented of *Adolphe*, the drawing-room novel was the novel of the times. It took in the modern hero who migrated thence with all his complexes and contradictions from romantic poetry. There was thus a natural bridge from the Cleopatra poem to the society tale. Its forte was analysis, psychological and social; the very existence of the hero in society became problematical. The genre was ideally suited to contrast convention and freedom, reflection and feeling, society and nature. The interpretation of Cleopatra's character and the presentation of a fatal choice were bound to be affected by this new context. The original poem had left the outcome of the action in doubt. The youth was the one in danger, although Cleopatra had been in a sense disarmed or defeated by his love. She had stepped out of her regal role. The question with Volskaya and Minsky is whether even the greatest *grande dame* is as complete a creature of society as the man of the world who fancies himself only its satirical observer. The answer in "Egyptian Nights" can only be guessed, but in "Guests" it is plain. Of course she is not. Chirpak-Rozdina refers to Liza's remarks in "A Novel in Letters" (1829) that while men's character changes with the intellectual fashion of the times, women remain true to feeling and nature.[9] The Princess declares of Volskaya, "Society still does not deserve such disregard from her." As for Minsky, "He did not like society, but did not scorn it for he knew that its approval was indispensable." By the third fragment of "Guests" he has already tired of Volskaya. In the society tale she has no real lover. Her love is an impossible dream for which only she is ready to risk everything; therefore it is she who is doomed. Her behavior is suicidal, as the sympathetic neighbor of Princess G. made clear by an image in the draft: "She will end badly. Looking at her I imagine a sleepwalker who is going along a roof—you want to call out to him and you do not dare; you do not know whether to wish him to awaken" (J. VIII$_2$, 548). Another variant of this layer reads, "going along the abyss." The awakening for Volskaya promises to be disastrous. Theoretically, an alternative outcome is possible: release of the sleepwalker from the spell could restore the victim. That will be the solution of the *Tales of Belkin* where the characters find, to their relief, that their romantic imaginings were simply a bad dream. But this is possible only where nature is taking its course, a solution practically excluded in the artificial society setting.

In "Guests" two conversations form a commentary to the society tale with its unconventional, romantic heroine. First, there is the long second paragraph which introduces the two observers, sitting apart on the balcony, a Spaniard and an unidentified Russian, evidently Minsky. Then, after Volskaya's entrance, come the predictions of two figures of authority in society, the Princess G. and her neighbor. We have society from the outside and from the inside, enveloping Volskaya's appearance. The two men, the Spaniard and the Russian, speculate about the northern and southern climates of love; in fine symmetry, they launch the subject of the "old quarrel between *la brune et la blonde*," as Minsky puts it. This sets the stage for the planned rivalry of Zélie and the provincial girl. Pushkin, of course, leaves open the question of *la brune et la blonde*, but it is the Russian to whom the dark, southern beauty appeals, "the swarthy, black-eyed Italian or Spanish girl, full of liveliness and southern languor." Volskaya has the southern beauty. We learn that the Russian is her romantic confidant. The effusive and courteous Spaniard feels romance in the air in the beautiful northern night. Minsky counters with a critique of the conventionality and hypocrisy of Petersburg society and its amours. This urbane banter has a philosophical undercurrent which of all the conversations reported alone fits it to be the general conversation which society lacks. But the two on the balcony quickly shift ground. "And the conversation took a most satirical turn"—that is, the comment becomes off-color. Thus, when Volskaya arrives, we associate her, in potential, with the most poetical and the most prosaic of loves. Still more important, her unconventional behavior must now be construed as a social statement.

The second conversation reports an exchange between the Princess G. and a certain gentleman, who here speaks first:

> —I admit that I sympathize with the fate of that young woman. There is a lot of good in her and much less bad than people think. But passions will be her ruin.
> —Passions! What a big word! What are passions? Aren't you imagining that she has an impetuous heart and a romantic head? She is just badly brought up... What lithograph is that? A portrait of Hussein-Pasha? Show me.

(VI, 562)

This passage is possibly still more significant than the conversation on the balcony for setting the terms of the new Cleopatra story. The man who says "passions will be her ruin" is speaking the language of the classic drama. This Cleopatra's fate could be tragic; *she* could be the object of compassion. "*Gromkoe slovo!*" retorts the lady—"Big words." It is no argument, of course, when a lady who casually inspects lithographs of a very real Hussein Pasha in a drawing-room scoffs at the reality of the passions. (The draft was even more uncompromising: there she flatly declared, "Passions do not exist" [J. VIII$_2$, 548.]) "An impetuous heart" and "a romantic head" are authentic attributes of Pushkin's Cleopatra. But Pushkin would be the first to agree that Volskaya has been badly brought up, though not in the sense intended by the queens of the drawing-room. With no other mental equipment than her romantic ideas she is about to run up against the reality of the society characterized by Minsky. Life as it is lived will never measure up to her fantasies, its satirist Minsky least of all, which is perhaps more a criticism of life as it is lived than of the "romantic head."

So in "Guests" we have the "Cleopatra" kernel where the crowd (*tolpa, gosti*) has emerged as a picture of society and where society and its critics are made articulate. But it will not do to identify

Pushkin entirely with the satirical conversation on the balcony or with the bluff talk which dispenses with romantic clap-trap. The mocking tone in which both are conducted is suspect. Minsky's superficial and cruel remark, "She is killingly funny," strikes a chilling final note in the first scene and characterizes Minsky himself to perfection. This leaves the question of Pushkin's relation to Volskaya. Quite simply, the author looks on her with compassion.

Pushkin's 1828 review of Baratynsky's dramatic poem, *The Ball*, a work remarkably similar to "Guests," confirms this view. This is a sort of society tale in verse. Belinsky called its heroine, Nina, "a demonic character in female form."[10] Like Pushkin's Cleopatra, Baratynsky's Nina has a vivid imagination. Nina wants to play with lives, but *her* moment of fate has come, "*poslannik roka ei predstal.*" Like Pushkin's Volskaya, she is threatened with the loss of her lover to a chaste young girl. Nina's fate resembles the probable fate of Volskaya: "My unhappy love is a punishment from above."[11] Baratynsky shows her a sympathy quite unlike the feigned condolences of the hack poet with which he affects to close the poem.

In 1828 Pushkin wrote the following appreciation of Baratynsky's new work. The inspiration behind "Guests" reads directly from it:[12]

This brilliant work is filled with original beauties and an unusual charm. With amazing art, the poet has combined in a swift tale the jocular and the passionate tone, the analytic and the poetic [metaphysics and poetry].

The poem begins with the description of a Moscow ball. The guests have gathered, old women ostentatiously dressed sit along the walls and look on the crowd with "stolid attention"...

Suddenly there is a stir, a rain of questions. Princess Nina has suddenly left the ball.

The hall is full of whispering:
"She has gone home!
Suddenly she felt unwell." "No, really?"
"Merrily whirling in the quadrille
She suddenly went pale!" "What's the reason?
Ah, my God! Tell me, Prince,
Tell me what is it with Princess Nina,
Your wife?"

"God knows," the Prince answers with husbandly indifference, taken up with his card game. The poet answers for the Prince. The poem comprises his answer.

Nina occupies our attention exclusively. Her character is wholly new, developed *con amore*, in broad terms and with amazing art; our poet has created for it a completely unique language and expressed in it all the nuances of his subtle analysis; he has lavished on her all his elegiac tenderness, all the charm of his poetry.

> Full of contempt for public opinion,
> Doesn't she mock
> Woman's virtue as
> A country affectation?
> Whom does she entice to her house:
> Isn't it inveterate lovelaces,
> And good-looking novices?
> Aren't people tired of hearing
> The tales of her shameless conquests
> And alluring liaisons?
>   But how her lively beauty
> Drew them all-powerfully to it!
>
> ...

In vain the poet sometimes adopts a severe tone of condemnation and reproach, in vain he speaks of her death with forced coldness, satirically describes her funeral for us and ends his poem in jest. We feel that he loves his poor, passionate heroine. He makes us share a painful sympathy for the fate of the fallen but still enchanting creature.

Arseny is the very one whom poor Nina had to have loved. He has a powerful hold on her imagination and, never completely satisfying either her passion or her curiosity, was destined to retain his fatal *ascendancy* over her to the end.

(VII, 83-86)

Actually, Pushkin's heroine and Baratynsky's shared a common prototype. In "Guests," Pushkin was drawing on his poems to Zakrevskaya whom he portrayed sympathetically as "the lawless comet," the passionate nature that flashes across the cold, northern sky ("The Portrait," III, 69). Zakrevskaya was a living embodiment of the romantic. As Petrunina has shown, the phrase "the lawless comet" is a reminiscence from *Melmoth the Wanderer* and attaches to one of its heroines, Immalee: "Immalee, child of nature, is opposed both to the demonic hero Maturin and to convention-bound Madrid society."[13] It has rightly been said that "Guests" reads like a gloss on the Zakrevskaya poems, the scattered episodes of a Pushkin society tale in verse.

The very fact that verse and prose settings of the Cleopatra material compete in 1828 shows that Pushkin was of two minds about sacrificing poetry to analytic prose. In the society tale he would equip his vivid theme with a social context, biographical motivation and the rest of the arsenal of realism. And he would pointedly confront Volskaya's romantic imagination with the "prose of life." But he actually needed to retain a tension, a combination of the poetic and the analytic such as he praised in Baratynsky. We began by seeing that much of the Cleopatra poem had been submerged in the opening of "Guests." The story, prose that it is, cannot conceal its poetic origins. The Zakrevskaya lyrics actually form a sort of mid-way point between the original poetic conception and prose. Pushkin attributes to Minsky, his man of the world, the role of confidant out of the lyrics. Of course, confidences can be seductive, and the poet is close to his "lawless comet," but as the confidant he retains his position as a "third person," retains his detachment. The confidant holds the germ of a narrator's interest in a story—thus "Guests" easily emerges out of the Zakrevskaya cycle, a story told to you, which might have been yours but was not. In "Guests," Pushkin divides the roles: he ascribes the detachment to Minsky while reserving the sympathy to himself, the author. Thus Pushkin the poet retreats into the narrator in 1828.

Whether or not to cast his heroes as poets was a question which vexed Pushkin more than once, as we know from the history of *The Bronze Horseman*. In "Guests" it is tantamount to asking whether the poets are the same as the heroes of our time, or perhaps their doubles. (If so, then as Mandelstam writes of his Parnok in "The Egyptian Stamp": "Give me the strength to distinguish myself from him."[14]) Pushkin finally answers yes when he substitutes the Petersburg poet and man of the world, Charsky, for Minsky, but the tension between Charsky and the improvisor, summed up by some as the realist poet versus the romantic, is already sketched out in Minsky's satirical postscript to the Spaniard's lyrical effusions. (The pairing begins, of course, with Lensky and Onegin.)

In 1828, neither hero in "Guests" is a poet, but many poetic elements are there. There is already a good deal of theater and a good deal of poetry in the opening of "Guests." At this point, Pushkin subtly suggests what he will later spell out. The story awaits the added dimension of art as a theme. In "Egyptian Nights" the salon is transformed into a private theater for the performance of the improvisor. In the 1828 story, all the guests have just come from the theater where a new Italian opera has been performed. The animation imparted by art lasts until social "order" is gradually established. But the *salle* (*zala*) in an important way replaces the theater—"the hall filled." And Pushkin is definitely thinking of society as a "stage" where dramas are performed. As he writes of Minsky, "He reappeared on the society scene" ("*Iavilsia on vnov' na stsenu obshchestva*"). These expressions are rarely ossified with Pushkin. The circles of guests are reminiscent of the tiers in an opera house. The guests settle down and we turn to the hero and heroine for the "play." We have moved from one society entertainment to another; society cannot conceive the dramas to be real where either art or life is concerned. It is because society is empty that art rushes in to fill the void. Like nature, art abhors a vacuum. "And the perusal of Parisian lithographs replaced general conversation." As against the lack of general conversation, we have the dialogue on the balcony (the two friends) and then the tête-à-tête (the two future lovers). Pushkin envisaged transferring the setting once more to the theater for Volskaya's second attempt at an explanation with Minsky (VI, 566).

The poetic current in "Guests" issues from what we might call buried poems. First, of course, there is the Cleopatra poem and in the second place the evocation of the magical Petersburg night ("he gazed with admiration at the clear, pale heavens..."). Volskaya ascends the stairs, or, more aptly, "rises," like the moon ("*Vol'skaia vzoshla*") and Pushkin closes the muted comparison by saying that her face was "as changeable as a cloud." Still, the mode of the society tale is overwhelmingly analytical. Thought and more thought was Pushkin's prescription for prose, after all (VII, 15). But when he praised Baratynsky's *Ball* for its combination of "metaphysics and poetry" he revealed something of his own aspirations. Eventually, "Egyptian Nights" would amply fulfill them.

The Context of 1828

In the larger context of Pushkin's work, the creative history of the 1828 "Cleopatra" and "Guests" is intertwined with that of *Poltava* and *Onegin*. To treat *Poltava* first, in it Pushkin attempted to join the epic tale of Peter's victory over Charles XII with the romance of Maria's love for the treasonous Ukranian *hetman* Mazeppa. In the love story, Pushkin deliberately returned to the manner and material of his southern poems, from which "Cleopatra," too, had originated.

Maria has reminded some readers of the "lawless comet," the woman of his poems to Zakrevskaya and the heroine of "Guests."[15] She is called sinner and criminal; her "unwomanly soul" is a match for Mazeppa's in rebellion. Her imagination is taken with his songs. In fact, Poltava's love story, the drafts to "Guests," and the 1828 "Cleopatra" have been shown to mesh.[16] *Poltava* was begun in April, 1828 with the historical line (characterizations of Peter and Charles and the significance of the war). Probably in August Pushkin made the transition to the character of Mazeppa and sketched a brief plan of the love story but broke off work to deal with the *Gavriliad* affair and to write lyrics, ending with "Happy he who is chosen at whim," part of the Zakrevskaya cycle. On the next two pages of the notebook Maria appears for the first time (Pushkin still refers to her as Natalya):

> And truly: in the Ukraine there is no
> Beauty equal to Natalya...
> Her eyes shine like stars,
> But seldom is a tear seen in them.
> Her lips glow like the dawn,
> But seldom, seldom and only for a moment
> Does a smile animate them—
> [Nature] strangely formed
> Her soul in the quiet of the steppes,
> And fate destined Natalya
> To be the victim of flaming passions.

(J. V, 186-88)

Pushkin finishes her portrait and indicates the theme of the bridegrooms, the last being Mazeppa. The following twenty pages of the notebook are filled with the manuscript of "Guests" which would appear to begin as a fair copy from an unknown previous first draft. Without interruption and in the same hand Pushkin returns to *Poltava* where he had left off, on the theme of the courtship.

Thus, Maria enters the notebook after the inception of "Guests" which ends in the discussion of Volskaya's possible lovers. Commentators have noted the outlines of "The Bridegroom" in Maria's introduction[17] (the courtship, her agitation, her absence from home, the fruitless questions of her parents). The resolution of her plot also falls into the bridegroom pattern, that of the feast which also passes sentence.

There is a cold dawning for Mazeppa after Maria pronounces judgment on him only to disappear as day breaks. This is the very thematic complex which underlies "Cleopatra": feast followed by execution, throne become execution block, feast of judgment. Translated into the society tale, "Guests," it spells retribution amidst the revels for Minsky, the impostor-lover who has captured Volskaya's imagination, then betrayed and ruined her. However, in *Poltava* Pushkin struggles for a balance. Apart from the mad lovers with their rebellion there is Peter to put down traitors and to make youth his teacher but not his master; in short, to restore order and a rational will. Thus, the love story of Mazeppa and Maria is placed in the historical frame of Peter's battles and mission. The moment for the writing of the second "Cleopatra" corresponds to Pushkin's "relapse" into the love story of *Poltava* after finishing with Peter's victory.

Izmaylov attributed Pushkin's amazing burst of energy in writing *Poltava* (1200 verses in a month) to his feeling that at that very time "his fate was being decided" (the climax of the *Gavriliad* affair).[18] It happens this way: Pushkin finishes *Poltava* in the fair copy on October 16, 1828. On October 27 he composes the dedication whose purpose, as Lotman has pointed out, is to redress the human balance with the severe historical line.[19] Next come materials for the epigraph from Byron. A little later, Pushkin returns briefly to "Guests"—"Minsky still lay abed . . ." One would have supposed that work on *Poltava* was finished. However, sometime before the middle of November, directly after this in the notebook, we find the beginning of the second Canto of *Poltava*, Maria's night conversation with Mazeppa. (Mazeppa reveals his ambitions to her; imagery of throne and execution block.) We do not know exactly when Pushkin capped Maria's final speech of condemnation with the recognition, "I took you for another, old man," closing the parentheses on the bridegroom plot (perhaps between the 16th and the 19th of October with still later revisions). He also added the epilogue (lines 424-71), "A hundred years have passed . . ." The dedication, the epilogue, two night scenes—and then, contemporary with the night scene from Canto Two, in a series of lyrics which follows in the notebook, we find the second "Cleopatra." The poem becomes one of the afterthoughts to *Poltava*.

Poltava does not form the only context for the Cleopatra material in 1828. The plan for the expanded "Guests," with its hero placed between two contrasting heroines, calls up many echoes. It resembles the shape of "The Blackamoor of Peter the Great," where Ibragim, like Minsky, also had to choose between two women. He dreamed of redeeming his past, of finding a fatherland and founding a family. This is what he returned from his journey to foreign parts to do. But for him the remedy failed. The plot sentenced him to repeat in Russia the farcical triumph of his Parisian society adventure, this time as a victim. "Guests" also bears a similarity to Pushkin's "Solitary Little House on Vasilevksky Island," told to a society audience one night in 1828 and written down by Titov. There, the hero is set between the demonic Countess I. and the angelic Vera. As Akhmatova wrote, "What if 'The Solitary Little House' is not just a piece of Petersburg Hoffmanniana but some sort of acknowledgment of one's life as fallen (cards, women, dissipation), as one which will end in madness if some Vera [Faith] does not save you."[20] The plan of "Guests" also contains a kind of preview for the final grouping of characters at the end of *Onegin*. The end of *Eugene Onegin* would be the dilemma which is both lock and key to so much of what followed in Pushkin, especially in his prose. To recall the situation, Onegin has returned from his journey: compare, in the draft to "Guests," Minsky's reappearance in society "having recently arrived from foreign parts." Onegin is no longer charmed by women of fashion; he has eyes for Tatyana alone, the provincial girl in Petersburg. But beside Tatyana, who is denied to Onegin, sits "the Cleopatra of the Neva."

> Charming in her carefree grace
> She sat by the table
> With the brilliant Nina Voronskaya,
> That Cleopatra of the Neva;
> And you would probably have agreed
> That Nina with her marble beauty
> Could not eclipse her neighbor,
> Blinding as she was.

> (*E.O.*. VIII, 16; 1830)

As Akhmatova succinctly remarked, this Cleopatra is the "anti-Tatyana."[21] What if the end of *Onegin* were only the beginning?[22] What if instead of Tatyana's resignation, however wise, we had another heroine's revolt?—Cleopatra's for instance, or Volskaya's, or Natasha's incipient rebellion in "The Blackamoor of Peter the Great," to name some contemporaries in Pushkin's manuscripts.

52

As Pushkin continued to work on *Onegin* even after supposedly finishing with it, Nina made her way again into Chapter VIII among the drafts and variants to stanzas XXIII-XXVI (this was in June, 1831). The stanzas describe Tatyana's ideal salon, its tone and perfect manners, as a setting for a motley and often satirized population. In the fair copy Pushkin generalized his observations on the women there, but omitted his remarks from the published text.

> The representative of society,
> And the one whose modest star
> Was some day
> To shine with humble happiness,
> And the one whose heart in secret,
> Bearing the punishment for mad passion,
> Nourished jealousy and fear,—
> Brought together by chance,
> Alien to each other in spirit
> They sat there side by side.

(V, 554)

The lovers sketched after the women would bear comparison with the three lovers for Cleopatra (stanzas XXV-XXVI). After them, in the rough draft, followed the entrance of Nina with the obvious attributes of the "Cleopatra of the Neva":

> Look, Nina comes into the hall,
> She has stopped by the door
> And *casts her abstracted glance*
> *Around the attentive guests*;
> ....
> *All are in rapture*, in the skies
> Before this magical picture...

(V, 556, emphasis added)

As we have seen, "Guests" in certain ways recapitulates or retells Chapter I of *Onegin*—the education of the heroes, the round of society entertainments. (The picture of high society looks back to Chapter I and, of course, ahead to Chapter VIII, as yet unwritten.) The fair copy of Chapter VII, prepared on November 4, 1828, contained stanzas comprising "Onegin's Album," the record of his earlier life in society. L.S. Sidyakov has noted the close connection between several of these and "Guests":[23]

53

Yesterday R.C. said to me:
I have wanted to see you for ages.
Why?—everyone tells me
That I will hate you.
What for?—For your sharp conversation,
For your frivolous views
On everything; for your barbed contempt
For everyone; but that is nonsense.
You may laugh at me,
But you are really not that dangerous;
And did you know till now
That you are simply—very kind?

. . . .

Yesterday at V's, leaving the feast,
R.C. flew like the zephyr. . . .
I parted the enamored crowd
Before the Venus of the Neva.

(V, 543-45)

In addition, *The Moscow Messenger*, in October of 1827, published some stanzas eventually omitted from the novel, "Women, or a Fragment from *Eugene Onegin*" (V, 528-30). They were written in October, 1824, contemporary with the first "Cleopatra" and originally cast as Onegin's preachings to Tatyana (V, 530). They recall youthful loves, a great love in the past, present disillusion with love—with love as society women understand and practice it.

Onegin, like Minsky enlightening the Spaniard, pities the man who expects to wake strong passions or real love in women. Lust is at the bottom of every attraction, and with women even lust is a mere whim. Such are the reflections of the man of the world; such is his conversation. In a variant stanza Onegin, again like Minsky, admits his youthful blunders, complains of slander and vows to set his position aright. Onegin's speech to Tatyana (or the prelude to it) and Minsky's commentary on Petersburg manners for the benefit of the Spaniard contribute more than character delineation. They have a similar and important role to play in their respective plots. The cynicism of the man of the world is a boast of invulnerability, and every boast is a hidden challenge to fate. Onegin answers Tatyana, "I will not love," and it is she and none other whom he will love hopelessly, as though by the vengeance of the implacable Aphrodite.

Minsky, for his part, will be forced to acknowledge the power of what he took to be a mere flirtation.

So the cynics find themselves involved in impossible adventure, unable to go forward, catapulted backward instead into the romantic past they had rejected. (The Cleopatra poem buried in the opening of "Guests" represents the element of suppressed romantic reminiscence.) The "realistic" society plot is bound to close upon itself and end with an involuntary recurrence of romantic love, the untimely revenge of repressed feeling.

Onegin, come full circle as society novel, contains the configuration of "Guests," *Onegin* nearing its end and returning to its beginning. If the plan of "Guests" anticipates the end of *Onegin* (the pairing of Tatyana and the Cleopatra of the Neva), the opening of the story looks back to certain Odessa stanzas which date to 1825 and reflect Pushkin's life of 1824. On first publication in 1827 they were announced as part of Onegin's journey. When Pushkin eventually printed these stanzas and others from the journey as a postscript to the novel, the effect was to close the circle that was begun in Chapter I when the poet and Onegin stood ready to travel together to foreign climes. In them, Pushkin unfolds the account of his Odessa day from noon to moon-rise, very like the chronicle of Onegin's day as told in Chapter I: a stroll, the casino, news or scandal of town or commerce, a Bohemian feast with friends, a night at the opera, hints of romance. It is the Italian opera, and Pushkin hails Rossini, the Orpheus of operatic song. Close after the intoxication of music come the charms of women at the theater, the seductive opera box with its languishing Cleopatra (Riznich perhaps) ("*A lozha, gde, krasoi blistaia...*" V, 208). The opera is over, but an Italian melody hangs in the air:

> But it is late. Quiet sleeps Odessa;
> Close and warm
> Is the silent night. The moon has risen,
> A light, filmy curtain
> Envelops the sky. All is still;
> Only the Black Sea pounds...

> (V, 208)

The moon rises and a light curtain overspreads the sky—it is impossible to say whether the curtain finally falls on the opera which has poured out into the streets or whether, as Russians say, this is already "an aria from another opera," the curtain veiling for modesty

55

the drama renewed by the pounding waves of the Black Sea. "Guests" takes up where these stanzas leave off. All the elements are there, the leaving the theater, the pair of heroes, the languishing beauty, the resonances of Italy—South projected against North, the unfinished drama.

When this group of motifs makes its appearance in "Guests" it represents a reminiscence. Indeed, the poem "Reminiscence" written on May 19, 1828, began with an analogous evocation of nightfall and ended, in manuscript, with a scene in which the hero, a prey to memories of the wrong dealt him by society in his youth, is suddenly confronted by the shades of two women who stand with lifted swords of retribution and offer him "the secrets of happiness and the grave" (III, 60, 459).

Thus, the Cleopatra story fits into *Poltava* on the one hand and *Onegin* on the other. Both contexts highlight what might be called the revenge of the romantic despite the quest for the real. In the story "Guests" the primary imaginative pattern is elaborated by an analytic intelligence to give it social, psychological and ideological dimensions. But since the intelligence belongs to an artist, even the ideas which animate the work find poetic expression. "Metaphysics and poetry" do begin to blend in the final reprise of work on "Guests" which took place in 1830. There we can even start to see how the form of the future "Egyptian Nights" was shaped by an argument which preceded it, an argument full of its own intellectual pathos.

"Guests" 1830: The Egyptian Tombs and the General Conversation

In 1830 Pushkin returned to the opening conversation in "Guests," seeking once again to frame or define a social and philosophical context for the society tale. The temptation is to see the 1830 fragment as an independent quasi-journalistic set piece.[24] This is far too simple. Here Pushkin writes political prose but develops it by artistic means: characterization, dialogue, image. The fragment only comes alive when viewed as an element of a literary work rather than as a fictionalized polemic. Pushkin's literary manner was quite capable of incorporating it. The conversation which forms the new fragment represents a development or continuation of the balcony colloquy begun in 1828 between Minsky and the Spaniard. Not to deny its real underpinnings, that candid conversation might well have been rehearsed at the dacha of the Count and Countess Laval.

Zakrevskaya was an intimate of the house. Nearby was a summer theater which performed Italian opera. Though the owners were of the *parvenu* aristocracy, literary figures flocked to their house where diplomatic news might break and European intellectual life could bypass Nicholas' censorship. In Paris, Laval had visited Chateaubriand, Constant and Madame de Staël.[25] But the conversation acquires full thematic significance in 1830. It points forward. In "Egyptian Nights" all these conversations are excluded and replaced by the staging of an improvisation which implicitly illustrates the problems explicitly discussed in 1828/30. The private conversations of "Guests" actually embodied what Pushkin significantly termed the "general conversation" which society lacked. The reader who successfully penetrates the indirection of "Egyptian Nights" must be attuned to the general conversation which went before it.

First of all, the new dialogue of 1830 witnesses the surprising origin of the Egyptian motif in the creative history of the cycle; it arose as one of the topics of the general conversation.

What is meant by the "Egyptian" of "Egyptian Nights"? In poetic terms, no one thing. Guided by the subject of the Cleopatra poem, the reader of the story naturally interprets the title to mean first something romantic like "Cleopatra's nights of love." "Egyptian" does pertain in some sense to Cleopatra, more poetically than historically. Historically she was a Greek queen descended from the Ptolemies who conquered Egypt, whose task it was to reign at Alexandria in an increasingly Roman world. "Egyptian Nights" could be said to show Pushkin's appreciation of such historical circumstances, at least in literary terms: his Cleopatra is a free agent whose story is told by the Italian improvisor following the Latin classics who molded her image for the West, and told in a setting which, like hers, is "Alexandrian." Poetically, if Cleopatra is "Egyptian" for Pushkin it could be according to the old commonplace—discarded in the notes to *Gypsies*—by which "Egyptian" meant "gypsy"; in other words, in the sense that Egypt belongs with the passionate South.

Still, the story is not called "Nights of Cleopatra, Queen of Egypt," but "Egyptian Nights." Further reflection will bring forth the parallel historical situation implanted in the plot through the device of repetition: the luxurious nights of the Alexandrian decadence are, of course, to be compared with the nights of contemporary Russian high society. The classical decoration of the poem "Cleopatra" in

1824 and 1828 had never been specifically Egyptian. Not until the 1835 reworking would Pushkin elaborate an Egyptian setting for Cleopatra, cosmopolitan Alexandria, Alexander's city of hellenized Egypt, breathing the generalized atmosphere of late antiquity. Thus the "Egyptian" of Pushkin's title refers to the Alexandrian nights which take place in Egypt and in a Russia conceived as a metaphorical Egypt.

However, although the Egyptian motif appears in a conversation which openly takes as its theme the nature of Russian society, the connection in which "Egyptian" first arises in the creative history of the cycle does not involve the Alexandrian decadence. The sphere of reference is the "Egyptian tombs." This dead Egypt underlies the metaphorical setting of the future "Egyptian Nights"; it is the negative element into which the story of 1835 is plunged.

The 1830 fragment contains but one image, this image of the Egyptian tombs, important because it focuses what the draft characterizes as Petersburg society's "powerful effect upon the imagination" (J. VIII₂, 540). Egypt figures not as a concrete historical or social milieu but poetically as the land of the dead, of dead souls. In the fair copy the passage reads as follows, with the Spaniard speaking first:

> [N]owhere have I felt myself so constrained, so ill at ease, as in *your accursed aristocratic circle*—Every time that I enter the drawing-room of Princess V.—and see those *mute, motionless mummies which remind me of the Egyptian tombs*, a kind of chill goes through me. *There is not a single moral Power among them, not one name impressed upon me by Fame—what, then, makes me quail?*
>
> *Their malevolence*—answered the Russian, that is a trait of our character—In the common people it comes out as mockery—in the higher circles as lack of consideration and coldness. (There is no point even speaking of the men.) Moreover, our ladies are very superficially educated and *nothing European occupies their thoughts.*—Politics and literature do not exist for them—Wit has long been out of favor as a sign of frivolity—What, indeed, can they talk about? About themselves? No—they are too well brought up. *They are left with a kind of domestic, trivial, private conversation, comprehensible only to a few—to the elite*—And the man who does not belong to this small herd is received as a stranger—not just a foreigner, but even one of their own.

(J. VIII₂, 41; emphasis added.)

Obviously only an alienated author could use such language. The last sentence quoted is the lesson learned on Pushkin's recent return from his unauthorized journey to Arzrum (May-October, 1829). Petersburg society, seen afresh from the outside, struck him as the Egyptian tombs: monolithic inertia, silence. The sentiments "nothing European occupies their thoughts" and "they do not recognize a single moral power" are characteristic westernizing reflections also reinforced by the ironic return from the East to "civilization." The awkward and isolated position of the stranger, with which the Russian sympathizes, later becomes the lot of the unfortunate itinerant improvisor who does not know what to make of the silent Russian audience. Likewise, the typical "malevolence" of society anticipates the emblematic meaning of the "Queen of Spades" as revealed by the epigraph to that other society tale—"secret ill will" ("*tainaia nedobrozhelatel'nost'*").

It was not hard to feel Petersburg as Egypt, to read Egypt into its atmosphere, its very architecture. The "Egyptian" Petersburg recalls Pushkin's famous characterization of the city in 1828—"Boredom, cold and granite," "*skuka, kholod i granit.*"[26] The colossal shapes of Egyptian monuments would put Egypt on the map of Pushkin's projected poetic journey, the culmination of his "Autumn" (1833). To the questions, "Hurrah! ... Where shall we sail? What shores / Shall we now visit?" answers included: "Colossal Egypt," "Where drowse the symbols of eternity, the pyramids." A sketch of the Colossus of Memnon materialized on the margin.[27] The Egyptian monuments echo the somnolent "colossal shapes" (*gromady*) of Pushkin's empty Petersburg streets ("... *iasny spiashchie gromady / Pustynnykh ulits,*" *The Bronze Horseman*).

Egypt implied a dead weightiness. We learn from the draft to the new fragment of 1830 that the image of Egypt emerged as the "objective correlative" of the French *imposant* which suggested itself to Pushkin as the *mot juste* for Petersburg society's "powerful action upon the imagination": "*Chto zhe tak sil'no deistvuet na voobrazhenie?*" "*Cherezvychaino khoroshii ton imeet takoe [imposant] strannoe deistvie.*" The image results when the active imagination comes to grips with "moral inaction": "*Aristo-kraticheskaia vazhnost' nashikh dam proiskhodit ot ikh nravstvennogo bezdeistviia*" (J. VIII₂, 540). The Egyptian society is as silent as it is ponderous. The mummies frighten the visitor by their mute impassivity.

59

The comment on the Egyptian tombs launches a tirade that questions society's ability to conduct the cultivated "general conversation." This makes the Spaniard's discomfort in Russia understandable and answers his first question, "What, then, makes me quail?" A moment later he asks a second question, "On what, then, is your so-called aristocracy founded?" This might seem only an opening for Pushkin to air his social grievances, a pretext for a genealogical disquisition, like the outburst in "My Genealogy"(1830) provoked about this time by Bulgarin. But the two questions are intimately related; the second is an extension of the first: for Pushkin, true aristocracy is based on a community consciousness which already transcends class and prepares an articulate public opinion. Pushkin is ironic about personal family pride. He writes of the "complacent carelessness" with which the Russian discusses his ancestors. The aristocracy interest Pushkin as the past creators of cultural values; genealogy makes history. As Pushkin claimed on another occasion, the family tree of kings is the history of the nation.[28] The new, created nobility have no depth of historical consciousness. They do not even listen to the nation's history as told to them by Karamzin. "*Proshedshee dlia nas ne sushchestvuet*" (draft, J. VIII$_2$, 543). The past simply does not exist for them, and this becomes a mark of their fundamental immorality: "*Neuvazhenie k predkam est' pervyi priznak dikosti i beznravstvennosti*" (J. VIII$_2$, 42).

Pushkin has arrived at an idea of what constitutes immorality independent of the standard by which society is ready to judge the Cleopatra-heroine of "Guests," Volskaya. If she was "badly brought up," then so, too, in a profounder sense, was society at large—empty, superficial and valueless. So the argument about the foundations of aristocracy completes the elements of a morality case. It also completes the Egyptian image which initiated the discussion, although Pushkin has ceased to call the valueless society Egyptian. But the Egyptian Petersburg had constantly been defined by negation: "There is not a single moral Power among them, not one name has been reiterated to me by Fame," "Politics and literature do not exist for us," and now, "The past does not exist for us" (the final version of the last remark reads "the spell of the past ... "). This recalls the modern retort of the countess in the draft to the 1828 "Guests": "Passions do not exist" (J. VIII$_2$, 548). This is the cumulative effect of the social criticism in "Guests." There is no moral power, not a single name known to fame, no politics or literature, no past, no passion.

"We are so positive, so practical," the Russian comments with meaning irony, "*My tak polozhitel'ny*." For the phrase translates the French *positif* and really signifies, "what nihilists we are," to use the word which the generation after Pushkin preferred. We acknowledge no authority and bow to no absolute values. We pretend that they do not exist. The capitalization of "moral Powers" and "Fame," which only the Jubilee edition refrains from normalizing, is the graphic sign of the absolute. "We are so positive" is the ironic nineteenth-century phrase which so often brings on a literary protest. In "Egyptian Nights" the point will be to assert, in the face of the Egyptian society, not only that passion exists in their midst—"Guests" did that—but also that the distant past exists to cast a powerful charm, that poetic genius exists to hold them enthralled, and finally that a moral power exists to demand a reckoning or a change of heart. In "Egyptian Nights" there is a real counterpart to Cleopatra in the audience. But she represents there not the ideal past of the ancestors present in a healthy nation, but rather the demonic past of the classical anecdote which comes to life in the drawing-room society. The first improvisation takes as its theme an absolute, the freedom of poetic genius. The second improvisation forces its listeners to contemplate the idea of Cleopatra's sentence on her lovers, though she only acts as the instrument of some moral power of retribution without being that power herself. The remark "We are so positive" can also bring with it into literature the protest of fantasy. The projected plot of "Egyptian Nights" is a poetic fiction which is imparted to the susceptible in a moment of theatrical illusion. Art pours into the vacuum of the "positive society," of the Russian Egypt.

Society is bored by its own emptiness—it welcomed Volskaya's childish animation as a distraction in the 1828 "Guests." A draft passage for the 1830 fragment suggests that what society needs is a "public conversationalist," a *razgovorshchik*, who will carry on the general conversation of which society is incapable as a performance:

> Everyone feels the necessity for general conversation—but where is it to be gotten—and who wants to be the first to take the stage [go on show]. Someone suggested hiring a conversationalist for the evening just as that poor pianist is hired for small balls.

(J. VIII₂, 541)

Compare Pushkin's letter to Vyazemsky of January 25, 1829: "We should have guessed it long ago: we were made for receptions, for

61

there you need neither intelligence, nor gaiety, nor general conversation, nor politics, nor literature" (X, 257).

These reflections reach back to a variant of the balcony conversation in the 1828 "Guests":

> Everyone tries to be respectably trivial with taste and propriety... Listen attentively to our conversations. Dry news from Shumla which you can read the very next day in the papers—chat about some mediocre new actor, and occasionally an off-color story told without the least verisimilitude.

(J. VIII₂, 546)

Just another off-color story told without verisimilitude is what the Petersburg audience expects from the theme "Cleopatra and her lovers" which the poet must transform.

The conversationalist first prescribed in "Guests" perfectly defines the later role of Petronius in "A Tale from Roman Life"; of Aleksey Ivanych in "Evening at the Dacha," and of his heir the improvisor in "Egyptian Nights." In "Evening at the Dacha," Aleksey Ivanych suggests Cleopatra as a theme and was to have recited from a friend's poem about her to stop the clamor "Oh, tell it, do tell it!" (VI, 602). The improvisor is cut out as a poor entertainer from the start; it is his function as the conversationalist which we should bear in mind. The 1830 fragment provides us with the terms of the general conversation about the spiritual death of Petersburg society which Pushkin and the poets conduct covertly in "Egyptian Nights" above the heads of their audience. It tells us both what is to be discussed and how it must be discussed.

Conversation, in fact, emerges as a kind of meta-theme connected with the Egyptian reflections of 1830. This is conversation about conversation. The draft tells us that the Spaniard heard in the Russian's talk for the first time in Petersburg a specimen of the "Parisian *causerie*" (J. VIII₂, 541). The whole passage perhaps reflects Madame de Staël's critique of the silence of Russian society in *Ten Years of Exile* and therefore her influential ideas on the difficult relation between literature and society in Russia. Pushkin, in one of his notes to *Onegin* (1830) pretends to turn a compliment on the "Eastern charm" of the Russian ladies of the aristocracy, a point of observation which turns out to have been based on Madame de Staël: "Our ladies combine education with politeness and a strict purity of morals with the Eastern charm which so captivated Madame de

Staël. See *Ten Years of Exile"* (V, 193). When the Spaniard sought in vain for Parisian *causerie*, Pushkin probably had these comments from Madame de Staël in mind:

> What we understand in France by the pleasures of conversation can hardly be found [in the Petersburg great houses]: the company is far too numerous for a moderately forceful conversation ever to be established. All high society has perfect manners; but there is neither enough education among the nobles nor enough trust among people who live continually under the influence of a despotic court and government to make it possible to know the charms of intimacy...
> ...[C]ertain Russian noblemen have tried to shine in literature and have given proof of talent in this career; but enlightenment has not spread sufficiently for there to exist a public opinion formed out of the opinions of individuals... Morever, every significant thought is always more or less dangerous in the midst of a court where everyone keeps watch on everyone else and where, more often than not, they envy one another. The silence of the East is transformed into amiable speech, but speech which does not ordinarily get to the bottom of things.[29]

Quasi-philosophical conversation was also typical of the "nights" genre, beginning with Batyushkov's "An Evening with Kantemir" where those present "philosophize about the North" and speculate on the fate of Asiatic Russia, to the later and equally speculative *Saint-Petersburg Evenings* of Maistre and the *Russian Nights* of Odoevsky. The nights have an intellectual content as well as a notorious seductive appeal. The European conversation in and about Asiatic Russia goes on during nights like these. But Pushkin begins to doubt the very possibility of making it public and by extension to question the viability of his society tale. Could literature replace the general conversation? Was society ready for it?

The 1830 fragment of "Guests" has an obvious satirical edge. Within the creative history of the cycle the general conversation "takes a satirical turn" beginning with the 1828 "Guests" ("*Razgovor prinial samoe satiricheskoe napravlenie"* [VI, 561]). Then "satirical" meant off-color commentary which implied freedom from conventional attitudes. By 1830 the basis for the social criticism becomes explicit. The satirical observation of high society in the 1830 "Guests" coincides with the high society scenes in Chapter VIII of *Onegin* (December 24, 1829—September 25, 1830),[30] where the "Cleopatra of the Neva," Nina Voronskaya, sits down next to Tatyana. The Egyptian motif was part of the satirical treatment. It has an interesting context in the larger conversation about ideas which was indeed just beginning to exist in Russia.

No doubt the image of the Egyptian tombs owes something to Chaadaev's historio-philosophical criticism of Russia, the subject of a continuing dialogue between the two writers. Chaadaev's first "Philosophical Letter" was dated "Necropolis [*i.e.*, Moscow], December 1, 1829." The letter began to circulate in manuscript in the early part of 1830. Perhaps Pushkin had already read it in March of that year when he wrote to Vyazemsky, "[T]he government is acting, or is minded to act, in the direction of European enlightenment ... I am thinking of launching into political prose" (X, 274-75). Pushkin mentions re-reading Chaadaev's manuscript in July, 1831, in a letter to the author and jests with him about returning it, saying "What will you do with it in Necropolis?" (X, 363).

In a wider perspective, both Pushkin and Chaadaev spoke as members of a common Europeanizing party. For them, Egypt was one of the lands of unhappy historical consciousness. In 1830, after his return from Arzrum, Pushkin wrote a review of Polevoy's *History of the Russian Nation* and made the well-known remarks:

> The greatest spiritual and political revolution on our planet has been Christianity. In this sacred element the world disappeared and was renewed. Ancient history is the history of Egypt, Persia, Greece and Rome. Modern history is the history of Christianity. Woe to the country which finds itself outside of the European system!

(VII, 143)

This historio-philosophical credo, which seconds Chaadaev's view, is a commentary on the "Egyptian tombs," where there has been no renewal, which lies outside the European system: "Nothing European occupies their thoughts."

If we trace back the ideological genealogy of the motif, we discover the existence of an older satirical tradition for the Russian Egypt in the Enlightenment. Pushkin follows the *conte philosophique* in which Egypt often stood for superstition and despotism. Ancient Egypt, according to this tradition, was ruled by a pack of corrupt and ignorant priests (*i.e.*, Jesuits) in league with cruel and rapacious Pharaohs (*i.e.*, unlimited monarchs). Voltaire, in "The Princess of Babylon" (Chapter VI), digresses to rejoice that Russia under the wise Catherine the Great has avoided the pitfalls of the exclusive and narrow Egyptian state. However, Voltaire's abundant flattery prompts the reader to make a more invidious comparison:

> Most lawgivers have had a narrow and despotic spirit, which has limited their aims in the lands which they have governed; each has regarded his people as being the only one on earth or as having to be the enemy of the rest of the earth... Thus the Egyptians, so famous for heaps of stones, were stultified and dishonored by their barbarous superstitions. They think the other nations unclean, they do not communicate with them, and, except for the court which sometimes rises above vulgar prejudices, there is not an Egyptian who would wish to eat of a dish from which a foreigner had served himself. Their priests are cruel and absurd. It would be better not to have any laws and to heed nature alone.... Our empress embraces entirely opposite projects...

Voltaire also has to contend with the literary tastes of the fictitious Egyptian Princess to whom "The White Bull" is dedicated, who has read *On Human Understanding* "by the Egyptian philosopher named Locke," and demands from him a moral tale.

The comparison could also work in another way, in the so-called Mirror of Princes tradition: an allegorical Egypt, the ideal state, was held up as an example to correct the abuses of the state as we know it. In Russia, Fonvizin translated Terrasson's Egyptian romance, *Sethos* (1731), as a transparent lesson to the heirs of Catherine the Great. As Vyazemsky commented:

> This work was particularly famed for the speech of the high priest of Memphis delivered at the funeral of the Empress, mother of Sethos. In this speech, under the pretext of praise for the departed, are clearly expounded the rules of pure political morality. In the words of D'Alembert, Plato would have recommended them to be read for the instruction of rulers; he also says that Tacitus would have admired this speech.[31]

Although Pushkin applies the word "Egyptian" to society, scrupulously avoiding the state, the Egyptian state was the predominant image of Egypt in the larger tradition. (Any attentive reader of Madame de Staël could not fail to have noticed the political origins of the Russian silence.) The Egyptian state, like other eastern forms of government, had no positive civic models to offer the Decembrist generation, unlike the classical civilizations of Greece and Rome. Winckelmann, their bible for norms in art history, thought much the same of Egyptian antiquities compared with the Apollo Belvedere. The pre-romantic taste which brought in sphinxes and Egyptian friezes as decorative motifs was an offshoot of the Empire style, inspired by Napoleon's imperial ambitions which led to the abortive Egyptian campaign.[32]

It would be tempting to attribute Pushkin's spark of interest in Egypt at least partially to a contemporary Egyptian fashion, all satirical tradition aside.[33] Egyptian antiquities did have a physical presence in Petersburg, both in museums and monuments. Egypt was also an intellectual presence, as interested minds followed the debate aroused by Champollion's decipherment of the mysterious hieroglyphs. The years 1828-30 were those of Champollion's own expedition to Egypt. Both the Decembrist Batenkov who reviewed Champollion's system and the conservative Russian Egyptologist Gulyanov had a range of literary acquaintance in common with Pushkin, from Bestuzhev and Ryleev to Chaadaev and not excluding the ubiquitous Grech and Bulgarin. There were present on the scene the combination Slavist-Orientalists, or even Slavist-Classicist-Orientalists, the universal antiquarians like Senkovsky who had published his Egyptian travels in 1820-21, and Olenin who corresponded with Champollion. At the Olenins where he was assiduous in 1828, at the Elagins, the Polevoys, or the Kireevskys, Pushkin might have heard Egypt discussed. It is known that Pushkin conversed privately with Gulyanov about Egyptology on at least one occasion, in December of 1831, leaving the scholar with a sketch of a pyramid as a memento of the visit.[34] Egypt was as fashionable in the drawing room and the diplomatic salon as in the halls of the Academy. The unriddling of the hieroglyphs was a scientific event which also stirred the imagination. The nascent discipline of Egyptology strove to lift unknown Egypt to the level of a classical civilization with a classic written culture. However, in the 1830's, Egypt was still interpreted for Europe through the ancient Greek historians and the Roman propagandists. Egypt itself offered no "names reiterated by Fame." The excitement of the discovery of Egypt may have been in the air, but when Egypt entered the history of "Egyptian Nights" in 1830, Pushkin turned to the image of the Egyptian tombs.

Chaadaev had commended Gulyanov's Egyptology to Pushkin as an example of what a Russian might do to win fame, in the hopes of seeing Pushkin, too, "initiated into the mystery of the times." This was in March-April, 1829:

66

My most ardent wish, my friend, is to see you initiated into the mystery of the times. There is no more distressing sight in the moral world than that of a man of genius who fails to comprehend his century and his mission...I find the name of my friend Gulyanov pronounced with respect in a weighty tome and the famous Klaproth conferring on him an Egyptian crown; I really believe that he has made the pyramids sway on their foundations. See what you can do for glory. *Cry out to heaven,* it will answer you.

(J. XIV, 44)

This calls to mind Napoleon's remark to his men just before the Battle of the Pyramids, "Soldiers, forty centuries look down upon you." However, as we have seen, Egypt was the last place where Pushkin thought to find moral powers, fame or immortality.

What, then, is the writer's relation to the "Egyptian" state of affairs in society? He is its satirist, its assailant, but he is also its ferment, the mover of that dead weight. As Delvig wrote to Pushkin, "No other Russian writer has moved our stony hearts as you have"(J. XIII, 110). In this, of course, Pushkin is greater than his ironic heroes, more than Minsky in 1828, or the Russian in 1830 as well as their partner, the Spaniard. When Pushkin came to "Egyptian Nights," he transformed these heroes into a pair of poets and made them the springs of the plot, not simply observers. One of the pair, the Italian improvisor, has the power to animate the assembly, as Cleopatra herself does in the original poem, where her voice and glance quicken the indolent revelers at the feast. But even the poets in "Egyptian Nights" are no more than characters; another, guiding consciousness informs the story. We know that the poetry of the improvisations began as Pushkin's own verse and must ultimately be referred to him. The larger design of the story is also his alone. Egypt does not figure in the 1835 prose text, but the title was devised by an author who remembered the Egyptian reflections of 1830. It was not so much the image of the Egyptian tombs as the meditations which it inspired that had an important future in "Egyptian Nights." The story is Pushkin's artistic challenge to the "Egyptian" state of affairs.

It was more than natural that the image of Egypt in the 1830 fragment was the Egyptian tombs. Egyptian referred to the funereal atmosphere of Petersburg society, ponderous and silent, whose denizens could be seen as the population of a necropolis. Egypt was the perfect metaphorical set for "Egyptian Nights." Land of the dead, of the buried past (in another context this meant the repressed reminiscence of a lost romantic love), Egypt was also the land of a

67

dead civilization, a moribund culture—the land of the eastern historical correspondence built upon the Cleopatra anecdote. The fragment of 1830 provides as direct a statement of convictions as Pushkin ever made, the kind of statement which he later eschewed, partly to be more persuasive, but also partly to conceal his true intentions when faced with a hostile social climate—the Egypt of "Egyptian Nights."

* * *

"Guests" 1830 forms the postscript to the Cleopatra cycle in its middle stage. Here Pushkin reaches the limits of the society-tale treatment. Perhaps he comes up against the impossibility of writing one to satisfy him given the Russian circumstances, or perhaps the time for writing such things has passed for him. This reprise falls at the crossroads leading to the late period in Pushkin—the end of *Onegin* as society tale intersected by the return from Arzrum. In the first months of 1830, Pushkin is active as a journalist for Delvig's *Literary Gazette*. Yet in the famous first Boldino autumn when *Onegin* was nearly completed, its political chronicle is burned or enciphered, while the *Tales of Belkin* alternate with the *Little Tragedies* like a pure confrontation of comic and tragic masks.

The middle period is to some extent the middle way in Pushkin, the approach to the mean, the "real," prose, a public voice. History, biography, philosophy and politics blending with plot and character. It anticipates literature in the full-blown nineteenth-century sense of the word, literature as the ideal general conversation. But Pushkin quickly moved through this stage. No doubt he continued to admire what he had praised in Baratynsky—the blend of "metaphysics and poetry," or anyalysis and imagination. But in the thirties he never again attempts to tell the Cleopatra story straight, or in ordinary prose, however sophisticated its simplicity. He always layers it, filters it through a story-teller, stylizes its language or makes subtle use of parody. The poetry re-emerges next to the prose. And the reader feels not that he is participating in the general conversation but that he is being initiated into a secret language or shown a triple-bottomed box, to use Akhmatova's terms.[35]

After all, the society-tale treatment was only one possible realization of the psychological paradox of "Cleopatra," the narration and conversations which framed it only one possible way of making sense of the suspended outcome, the fates which hung in the balance.

III

STYLIZATION AND PARODY: THE PATH TO "EGYPTIAN NIGHTS"

The Third "Cleopatra"[1]

The Cleopatra poem did not remain a fixed center for new prose frames. Fittingly, it, too, was stylized and thus moved into the repertoire of late Pushkin. There is more than one way to read the artistic effect of this stylization. But first some facts.

In 1835 Pushkin reworked the "Cleopatra" of 1828, although readers of "Egyptian Nights" would not suspect it, since the accepted text reproduces precisely the 1828 poem. Tomashevsky even wrote that it is permissible to speak not just of two versions but of two works on a common theme.[2] The third "Cleopatra," as I will call it, was specially tailored to the requirements of "Evening at the Dacha," the revival of "Guests." Moreover, work on the new version was not finished; so all in all it cannot be fitted into the text of "Egyptian Nights." This 1835 "Cleopatra" took a unique form combining prose and verse, suitable for the presentation of poetry by a method which mixes paraphrase and excerpts. The non-poet Aleksey Ivanych employs this to represent the creation of his poet-friend.[3] ("I suggested that ** make a poem out of it, he started but abandoned it.") Pushkin might have chosen to versify all of this for the second improvisation in "Egyptian Nights." A fragment of the new material, "Now day is already fled," the poetic equivalent of one prose section, is often appended to the 1828 text printed in "Egyptian Nights" (a situation which Tomashevsky justly deplores as an unwarranted contamination of texts).[4]

The Cleopatra improvisation, by tradition and by tradition only, stands as Pushkin's poem of 1828. Pushkin was perfectly capable of inserting an old poem into a new text; he did it in 1835 with "A Legend" for "Scenes from the Days of Chivalry." But he started the year by writing poems *ab ovo* for his "Tale from Roman Life"; he wrote a new "Cleopatra" for "Evening at the Dacha"; he revised "Ezersky" for the first improvisation. We cannot simply assume that he intended the 1828 "Cleopatra" for "Egyptian Nights." Pushkin did rewrite "Cleopatra" in 1835, and in our capacity not as editors but as readers we should take note of the new directions which he sketched out, not only in the context of "Evening at the Dacha" but also in potential for "Egyptian Nights." The fair conclusion remains that Pushkin continued to develop the poem even as he incorporated the Cleopatra idea into different prose settings ("Tale from Roman Life," "Evening at the Dacha," "Egyptian Nights").

As Tomashevsky noted, some parts of the "second work on a common theme" coincide with parts of the 1828 poem while others are entirely new.[5] In it, by comparison with the earlier Cleopatra poems, Pushkin passes from an expansion of the setting (palace and chorus) directly to the moment of Cleopatra's reverie. Evidently, he was working from memory. It is unclear where he would have put a new psychological study of satiety organized around the theme of Cleopatra's days and nights. Another lead-in reads "Cleopatra rouses from her reverie," which is followed only by the challenge section of the old poem without the oath, the lots or the acceptance by three lovers. The text of this passage does not correspond exactly with either previous version; apparently it, too, was supplied from memory. Pushkin transferred elements of the oath into Cleopatra's new meditations, perhaps out of unconscious poetic economy. We must bear in mind that this new version is far from complete.

The plot is taken no further in 1835 than before. As Tomashevsky stressed, "Cleopatra" is still deliberately open-ended. Its fragmentary nature, similar to that of an open question, was important to the conceptions of all the 1835 prose works organized around it. Pushkin explicitly mentions this in "Evening at the Dacha" where the poet "began but abandoned" the subject. However, if poetic fragments formed part of Pushkin's repertoire, prose fragments never had any independent value for him. While the poem "Cleopatra" is complete, the story "Egyptian Nights" remains unfinished. Therefore, to understand better the possible destination of the prose material, we must get a sense of the poetic moments embodied in the third "Cleopatra."

Once he had established the text, Tomashevsky limited his substantive commentary to the new picturesque style of certain descriptions based on Plutarch. He considered the stylistic orientation to be realist, historicist, objective:

> Pushkin is avid for archaeological details. He reproduces the décor of the feast, dwells on colorful details of the court life of the Egyptian queen...

70

In these descriptions Pushkin strives for the accurate recreation of a historical style...

Comparison of the stylistic treatment of the Cleopatra plot in 1824 and 1835 shows how eleven years has changed Pushkin's artistic system. The historical elegy... is transformed into an objective narration...

In the first version the story of Cleopatra is told as a psychological paradox with no correlation to place or time of action. Here [in the 1835 "Cleopatra"] the same story is presented as an integral part of the historical characterization of an era. Cleopatra is not just an exceptional character, not just a distinctive incarnation of extreme passion in all its depravity; here Cleopatra is the queen of Egypt in the period of its political decline when all this luxury does not bespeak the might of the state but rather its imminent end. The theme of satiety comes to the fore as the psychological characterization of the era being described.[6]

The point about the extension of psychological characterization into a historical characterization of the age is well taken. Such is Cleopatra, such is the Decadence. As for Pushkin's aesthetic system, however, Tomashevsky's conclusions are based on the mistaken premise that "details" spell objectivity and that the artistic problem is one of description. Pushkin is not necessarily striving for mimetic realism, "the exact reproduction of a historical style." He may well be using style as a sign, for its imaginative effect. The style here is palpable—the piece is stylized. It seems to say: "see how vivid, see how real," not "this is how it was in Alexandria." Tomashevsky's reading is also incomplete. He had only one point of interest—the "archaeological details"—and fixed on Plutarch to explain them. He saw historical Alexandria coming to life before him and forgot Petersburg, the unspoken analogue. Consistently, he read realistic cues where others would read romantic. Without meaning to, he reduced the 1835 poem to a museum piece.

Let us try to complete and revise the picture. We remember that the poem adapted for "Evening at the Dacha" consists of paraphrase interspersed with verse excerpts. Pushkin added an opening cityscape which functions as an extension of the two lines prefaced to the original "Cleopatra." He now moves from a viewpoint outside the palace to the feast within. The setting, as we will see, is Alexandria-Petersburg; it carries the Petersburg theme. Then we come to the new description of Cleopatra's feast. These two passages do work together as ways of objectifying the psychological themes of the elegy, but they are balanced against another, verse passage which develops the inner motivation for Cleopatra's sadness, her satiety. This follows from a prose paraphrase of her meditative gloom which ends with the question "Why does she grieve?", a question which the poems of 1824 and 1828 made no attempt to answer. We no longer read of Cleopatra's softened emotion (her *umilenie*)—the paraphrase does not reach that point—but we hear of her sufferings and longings. ("She wanders, longing, now and then ... In vain the heart in her dully suffers, it thirsts for unknown pleasures; weary, sated, she is ill of apathy.") Clearly, the poem "Cleopatra" in 1835 is something more than historically concrete or specific. What new descriptive material there is does more than just give the scene visual presence or support the historical theme of the Decadence by its sumptuous luxuriance. It also acts to create a fabulous atmosphere around Cleopatra's nights.

Already Alexandria is not just Alexandria. It suggests Petersburg, and an enchanted Petersburg at that. The opening city-scape in the text of "Evening at the Dacha" varies the erotic nightfall scene with which we are familiar from the history of "Guests" and the poem "Reminiscence." "Dark, sultry night enfolds the African sky; Alexandria is asleep, her squares are silent,her houses darkened." The keynote is African since the theme is Cleopatra's alter ego, her southern city. "Distant Pharos burns solitary in her wide harbor, like a lamp at the head of a sleeping beauty." However, the lighthouse, the harbor, the very sphinxes reflected in the water all bespeak Petersburg.

As in a tale from the *Arabian Nights*, three hundred youths serve the guests, three hundred maidens pour the wine, as three hundred black eunuchs keep watch. This is to be Aleksey Ivanych's Egyptian anecdote, so the eastern, Egyptian atmosphere of stagnation and heaviness is conveyed by a newly invented motif of motionless air waiting for a breath of wind. This is developed over the whole third paragraph:

A porphyry colonnade, open from the south and north, awaits a breath of the east wind; but the air is motionless—the fiery tongues of the torches burn motionless; the smoke of the braziers rises straight up in a motionless stream; the sea, like a mirror, lies motionless at the pink steps of a semicircular staircase. The guardian sphinxes reflect in it their

72

gilded claws and granite tails... only the songs of the zither and the flute make the flames, the air and the sea tremble.

(VI, 604-05)

Perhaps the enchantment owes more to an evil spell. Music alone "shakes" the immobile elements of this world—fire, air and water. Art as a mover compares with nature's mover, the wind. Art is rhymed with feeling (*iskusstvo* with *chuvstvo*); its function is to animate. The theme of the first improvisation in "Egyptian Nights," of the private conversation between poets, is precisely "the wind that bloweth where it listeth" ("*Zachem krutitsia vetr v ovrage...*"). The second, Cleopatra improvisation is meant to stir the company gathered that night, conveying motion (that is, emotion) to the crowd, just as Cleopatra has "animated" her feast and made hearts "shudder" with passion. This dynamic role of art in the 1835 text belies the interpretation of Pushkin's intentions as soberly "plastic" and "classical."

In fact, the rhythmic periods written for the introduction to the Cleopatra poem suggest not so much the Latin classics as they do ornamental prose. It seems quite likely that Pushkin fashioned the style of such a rhapsode's prelude after models in the French romantics, whose importance for Pushkin Tomashevsky often noted, but in other connections. It was Lednicki who clearly pointed in their direction, chiefly with reference to the repetition plan of "Egyptian Nights" which reminded him of several aspects of Jules Janin's *Barnave* (1831).[7] Lednicki speaks of the "not only solemn and ornamental, but even impressionistic style of this fragment." He refers the reader to chapters in Janin.[8] Perhaps he meant specifically:

> Alors dans le ciel lacté, entre deux brises froides et sonores, quand la galère d'ivoire aux voiles de pourpre a cessé de se balancer dans le fleuve, on entend dans les airs une musique qui n'est pas de la terre, et qui se prolonge comme un long soupir. Cette musique, c'est Bacchus qui dit adieu aux convives.[9]

We might compare another page of French romantic prose, this time from Jules de St. Félix's *Cléopâtre: Reine d'Égypte* which Pushkin acquired in 1836:

> Une nuit, les grands sphinx, placés au bas de l'escalier de marbre qui descendait jusqu'à la mer, étaient battus par les coups de vent, et leur

73

tête de granit ruisselait sous une poussière humide. Le palais de Ptolémèe Philadelphe recevait dans ses portiques les lueurs blafardes des éclairs qui se croisaient au loin sur l'eau ténébreuse. Le phare de Sostrate Gnidien jetait aux nuées sa longue flamme, comme un serpent monstrueux qui darderait sa langue vive et rouge. Les rochers du Lochias brisaient en écume les flots marins, et par intervalles on distinguait sur le balancement des ondes quelques galères nageant à force de rames et revenant de Canope, malgré tant de signes funestes.

Or, à une galerie du palais ptoléméen, une femme contemplait la nuit, la tempête, le phare et la ville d'Alexandrie. Cette ville était à elle; à elle étaient ces deux ports, ces grands navires enchaînés; à elle les rives sablonneuses, les régions fécondes, les déserts sans borne, toute l'Égypte.[10]

If we note the fact that *Barnave* was mentioned in the drafts to "Evening at the Dacha" in the same breath with other "new novels," the "archaeological detail" of the passages of 1835 appears more under the aspect of romantic exotica.

It is only after the evocations of enchanted Alexandria, the fairy-tale feast and the heavy air that we return to the old Cleopatra poem and the queen's reverie amidst the feast. We immediately meet the next innovation in the old schema, according to the reconstructed text of "Evening at the Dacha," a new fragment of psychological portraiture ("Why does sorrow oppress her?"). It establishes more clearly the heroine's dividedness, the tension between Cleopatra as queen and goddess of love and Cleopatra as woman. (In the original elegy Cleopatra as woman would have spared the youth whom she was obliged to destroy according to her royal oath.) It was mainly to this end that Pushkin introduced the picture of Cleopatra's barque out of Plutarch and Shakespeare which so impressed Tomashevsky, and then (in draft) the scene of Cleopatra wandering forlorn in her private gardens. The situation of the Decadence is something subjectively felt, not just objectively observed, and the "classical" proves to be chiefly an erotic atmosphere.

> Now over the waves of the gray Nile
> Beneath the shade of a magnificent sail
> In her gold trireme
> She glides like a young Venus.
> Before her eyes incessantly
> Feasts follow upon feasts,
> And who has penetrated in his soul
> All the mysteries of her nights?...

74

In vain! the heart in her dully suffers,
It thirsts for unknown pleasures—
Weary, sated,
She is ill of apathy—

(VI, 605-06)

This section, printed in the text of "Evening at the Dacha," was revised from a draft which included a remarkable harem scene, placed after the line "She glides like a young Venus":

Weary with longing she wanders
In her gardens; she enters
The secret chambers of the palace,
Where the key of the gloomy eunuch
Guards handsome slaves
And chastely passionate youths...

(VI, 740)

The buried southern poem emerged briefly here. No doubt the material was too scandalous for the fictional audience of "Evening at the Dacha," for Pushkin did not work it into the cleaner copy. However, without it the "In vain!" of the next section loses its motivation. The pleasure gardens are a magnification of the humbler garden in which a sentimental heroine communes with her feelings, according to literary convention. Cleopatra as woman, the woman whom her hieratic setting cannot touch, is the new dimension to Pushkin's treatment. Cleopatra is a dreamer; after this passage she "awakens from her reverie."

Pushkin is making his contribution to the Cleopatra legend, following Shakespeare more than his source Plutarch,[11] and in much more than the details of the barque scene. It is Shakespeare's Cleopatra who is transformed in the last act of the tragedy to say of herself, "I have immortal longings in me" (v.2.278-79). It is she also who chooses suicide after she has brought Antony to ruin and death. Historically, the "Society of Inimitable Enjoyers of Life" which Cleopatra had formed with Antony and their friends became the "Society of Companions in Death." It is also Shakespeare's Cleopatra who foresees that the Romans will make scabrous propaganda of her story:

Saucy lictors
Will catch at us, like strumpets, and scald rimers

75

Ballad us out o' tune; the quick comedians
Extemporally will stage us, and present
Our Alexandrian revels. Antony
Shall be brought drunken forth, and I shall see
Some squeaking Cleopatra boy my greatness
I' the posture of a whore.

(Antony and Cleopatra, v.2.213-20)

Heroism went out of the world with Antony—this is Cleopatra's predicament in Shakespeare's last act where their romance has become a dream. "I dreamt there was an Emperor Antony" (v.2.76). This predicament is the point of departure for all those later versions of the Cleopatra story which test modern man against the dream. Pushkin's poem does not need to incorporate the plot of Shakespeare's *Antony and Cleopatra* to stand in its line of descent, Cleopatra after Antony.

It is interesting to compare the conception of Pushkin's Cleopatra with another contemporary one. Heine appraised Cleopatra from a kindred point of view in a sketch for his "Shakespeares Mädchen und Frauen," 1839. There, he compares her with the modern heroine Manon Lescaut and calls her "that Parisienne of antiquity." He sees her as a living paradox, both "too good and too bad for this world." *The* characteristic scene of Shakespeare's play for Heine seems to have been that in which Cleopatra interrogates the eunuch about passion (i.5.). Heine admires her wit and imagination, but the final joke is on her. She is a living, warm-blooded queen in the Land of the Dead. "How witty God is," is the poet's final word.[12]

Pushkin's Cleopatra, too, is a dreamer and also the only "real" person in her all-too-real world. It is the paradoxical "reality of the dream" which actually dictates Pushkin's stylistic approach. In telling the Cleopatra story, Aleksey Ivanych, the "conversationalist" in "Evening at the Dacha," refers to it as "*to skazanie o Kleopatre*," the "relation," what is told of her by way of historical legend. According to Aleksey Ivanych the *skazanie* was the subject of a *poèma*, a romantic narrative poem, which his poet-friend left unfinished. We have seen how a situation which might have come from *The Fountain of Bakhchisaray* surfaced in a draft. Aleksey Ivanych prepares us for Pushkin's auto-reminiscence, his reworking of an old poem. Contrary to Tomashevsky's view, Pushkin has not arrived at an entirely different aesthetic system. He deliberately looks back, in fact. The question is, why? How are we to take it? For "Egyptian Nights," complicated by the figure of the improvisor, the answer generally given is that Pushkin parodies the romantic style and romantic poet who represents a rejected earlier self. The auto-reminiscences could well support another conclusion. Perhaps what Pushkin does is rather to update and justify the romantic strain in his work.

A critical voice parries: if the 1835 "Cleopatra" is romantic, can it be meant seriously? If this is stylization and not Pushkin's own voice, does that not mean that it strikes a false note? I think not. Our perspective on the poem has been distorted by the choice of the 1828 "Cleopatra" for the text of the improvisation in "Egyptian Nights." We perceive it as "the old romanticism," while it was perhaps intended to convey a timeless romanticism. Let us answer with another rhetorical question. Would Pushkin elaborate this sequence for the sake of ornamental exoticism or even to criticize its style? No, Pushkin needs to create a particular pathos. What the stylization communicates is that its language is an objectively available medium, not just a mode of personal expression. The writer wants the style to carry meaning in his work, without having it referred to his mental state. The mode is romantic, when the work requires it to be. As for the French sources, they do not detract from Pushkin's use of them. He means the stylization to be potent, to project the "reality of the dream."

The third "Cleopatra" shows Pushkin rethinking and deepening his original poetic idea. This is particularly true of the way in which the stylization brings history into the poem, less for the sake of documentation or description than for artistic effect. History reinforces the "psychological paradox" springing from Cleopatra's divided nature. The original elegiac Cleopatra has been motivated historically, her psychology becoming that of the Decadence. Tomashevsky was right in emphasizing this. "Archaeological details" aside, his definition of the historical theme makes a difference to the interpretation of "Egyptian Nights." It brings out the defects of Bryusov's reading of the story which misjudged Pushkin's treatment. Bryusov stressed contrast, the contrast between an ideal wholeness and present spiritual dividedness. He attached the quality of wholeness to the actually complex world of late antiquity and severed the modern world from his "ancient" one. Pushkin's art alone preserved the harmonious spirit of antiquity, and the god whose approach the improvisor felt was, for Bryusov, Apollo.[13] But he ignored the divided nature of Pushkin's Cleopatra who belongs to the era which she represents—her ennui and longings. He refused to associate modernity with any image of antiquity. Yet we must admit that the analogy between two decadent times which Tomashevsky prepares in his interpretation of the Cleopatra poems may turn out all the worse for the modern world, if even by comparison with the genuine decadence of ages past ours is a pale imitation. Tomashevsky better defines the historical terms, but the terms do not give the slant of the comparison. Perhaps Bryusov with his neo-romantic tastes had a better feel for the poetry of history.

Tomashevsky's approach is historicist, but Pushkin is not attempting to write historical fiction here. The poem is historically true only in the sense of being faithful to the spirit of an epoch poetically conceived. Pushkin has not discarded Aurelius Victor's anecdote for Plutarch's history writing. "Historicizing" the Cleopatra poem is finally Pushkin's way of bringing home the reality of the passions to an audience for whom they simply did not exist ("*Strasti—gromkoe slovo.*" "*Strasti ne sushchestvuiut.*") His object was less to localize the old psychological theme than to pave the way for its expanding relevance, on the axis Alexandria—Petersburg. Characteristically for all the 1835 fragments, the subject is treated as "romantic" in its very "realism."

"A Tale from Roman Life": The Route of Stylization

The plot of "Evening at the Dacha" suggests the repetition of the Cleopatra anecdote in Petersburg society; this might be said to vary Pushkin's aims in *Count Nulin* where he "parodied Shakespeare and history."[14] Certainly the fate of the Cleopatra material in its various prose incarnations after 1828 depends on Pushkin's great attraction to parody which proved even stronger than his undoubted pleasure in stylization. (By parody I mean any creative reworking of familiar material in a different style, not necessarily one aimed at lampooning or criticizing the original.) We have discussed the preparation of the third "Cleopatra" for the society story "Evening at the Dacha" as though a contrasting modern style were the only possible frame for the theme. In fact, Pushkin had previously envisioned a Cleopatra story as part of a work to be executed entirely in stylization known as "A Tale from Roman Life." Alternatively, it is identified as "Caesar was Traveling," according to the first words of the extant draft. Its plan includes the point, "About Cleopatra—our reflections on the matter." In 1835 Pushkin wrote poems to fill other empty spaces in his "Tale," bringing him up to the Cleopatra theme. (The mix of prose and verse in this work is determined by Pushkin's imitation of its hero Petronius' *Satyricon*. By extension, Aleksey Ivanych's poet-friend and the Charsky in 'Egyptian Nights'" are latter-day Petronius figures.) The poems are dated January 6, 1835. For reference, "Evening at the Dacha" is dated, only roughly, to "the first half of 1835, before 'Egyptian Nights.'"[15] The plan for the Roman tale, found in the middle of the manuscript of "Caesar was Traveling," belongs either to 1833 when Pushkin first began his story or to 1835.[16] In any case, the idea of continuous stylization antedated 1835 when the plan was current. The whole of the fragment "Caesar was Traveling" leads up to the Cleopatra story, yet at this point Pushkin stopped short and the next piece which he did on that theme was for "Evening at the Dacha" which provides a contemporary frame. I would now like to deal with what "A Tale from Roman Life" contributed to Pushkin's ideas of late antiquity and to suggest why stylization was rejected when the story came to a decisive point with Cleopatra.[17] The stylization, which Tomashevsky singles out as the greatest innovation in the third "Cleopatra" (calling it "archaeological detail"), is only a survival of an element which operates under strict limitations.

For the themes of satiety and historical decadence grafted onto the Cleopatra poem go back to the plan for the "Tale from Roman Life": "reflections on the fall of man, on the fall of the gods—on the general lack of faith." The plan lays bare the historical perspective underlying late developments in the Cleopatra material as did "Guests" 1830. "A Tale from Roman Life" is the first extension of "Guests" fulfilling the need felt for the "conversationalist." Petronius tells his stories to an audience of friends gathered at a villa. The stories fall into the required satirical vein, for in the course of them Petronius dictates his *Satyricon*. Like "Guests" 1830, "A Tale from Roman Life" reflects Pushkin's mood after the return from Arzrum; it begins at the end of a journey. Catastrophe has overtaken the traveler Petronius in the shape of a messenger from Caesar bearing dread news ("Caesar's command to return to Rome and there await the decision of his fate"). Perhaps this distantly reflects the biographical fact that Pushkin suffered official displeasure for the journey to Arzrum, undertaken without permission. Petronius gives his friends leave to depart with an aphorism about "the traveler"

("The traveler rests beneath the shade of an oak on a clear day . . . ";
variant: "our journey is at an end"). Petronius is to find death in a
rented villa, which is home to no one, whose owner is presumably
exiled and whose family statuary can receive no piety, where the
inscription on the threshhold, "*Vale!*," rings ironically. One further
point of contact with the mood of 1830: in the draft (1833) Pushkin
placed Egyptian objects around Petronius. He was carried in an
Egyptian litter (*egipetskaia kachalka*), the tent under which the
company feasted each night was Egyptian (*slugi stavili egipetskii
shater*) and an Egyptian lamp burned by Petronius' bedside
(*egipetskaia lampada*"). (See J. VIII$_2$, 931, 933.) Pushkin was
building up to the Egyptian-*Roman* nights. We remember that
Pushkin's first source was Aurelius Victor. The Egyptian anecdote
had not just a Roman transmission, it had a Roman raison d'être and
a Roman author. It was a story made for the Rome of the Empire;
now Pushkin gives it a Roman setting. But Aurelius Victor retreats
behind Nero's arbiter of taste, Petronius.

The "Tale from Roman Life" is far from being just an embryonic
historical novel demonstrating to us yet again Pushkin the realist
before his time. Petronius' *Satyricon* is one of the most sophisticated
models possible for a frame narration with multiple anecdotes and
story-tellers, even more complex than Janin's *Barnave*, whose theme
and structure may have contributed to bring the *Satyricon* to the
foreground for Pushkin in 1833. In any case, "A Tale from Roman
Life" is the first of the works, characteristic of the late phase of the
Cleopatra cycle, in which the Cleopatra poem, after being submerged
into "Guests," re-emerges in coordination with a frame. This is
consistent with the genre of the *Satyricon*, Menippean satire, which
mixed prose and verse while combining all manner of subjects to
project the picture of a universal but sceptical mind.[18] This was an
attractive vehicle for Pushkin after *Onegin*.

The "Roman Tale" shows the evolution of Cleopatra's "pair,"
the lover/poet, just as the third "Cleopatra" shows the development
of the heroine herself. Petronius' initial situation anticipates the
Cleopatra poem, his story of Cleopatra only serving to focus what
has already become his personal situation.[19] The pleasure feasts of
the traveling party who turn night into day and day into night, the
sentence which Petronius calmly accepts from Nero's messenger to
the horror of the onlookers—all are derived motifs. The erotic
anecdote has lost plot value—it has become matter for philosophical
discussion about the relation to death which it implies. ("About

Cleopatra—our *reflections* on the matter.") As the story is structured, Petronius is cast as Cleopatra's lover, but only in a figurative sense. That is, he accepts her challenge as a matter of principle, for he determines to die at the end of the time which he allots himself. Characteristically, execution, the undeclared will of Caesar, like Cleopatra's decree in the poem, has been internalized as suicide. When he courageously chooses the death imposed upon him by Nero, Petronius comes as close as possible to redeeming his situation. While restoring the plot interest, "Evening at the Dacha" will adopt the solution of suicide. Petronius' fate is fit for the end of a tragedy, the end of a pursuit by the Furies, for after accepting his sentence he rests in a grove dedicated to the Eumenides. Pushkin has placed Petronius the poet in an unspecified nemesis plot. The Eumenides prevailed over Apollo himself, the patron of the grove in a first variant; they and not he embody the spirit of the place—a weighty substitution. It is as though Cleopatra with her revenge upon men had become the muse of retribution.

If Petronius understands the condition imposed in the Cleopatra poem, it is because he has much in common with its heroine, as Minsky had with Volskaya in "Guests." The characterization of Cleopatra in the 1835 poem repeats Pushkin's appraisal of Petronius in the words of the Roman poet's young friend: "Life could offer him nothing new; he had known all the pleasures; his feelings drowsed, dulled by habit." Spokesman for the theme of "the fall," of decadence, Petronius knows its psychology from the inside. After he has recited the anacreontic ode on age, pleasure and the finality of death, the "cloud of reflection" (*oblako zadumchivosti*) familiar from Cleopatra's reveries crosses his face.

As Chernyaev pointed out, Pushkin developed his Petronius characterization polemically, applying a corrective to the critical portrayal of Petronius in Tacitus' *Annals*.[20] The Latin stylization of "A Tale from Roman Life" puts Pushkin literally on a par with Tacitus as well as with Petronius; it makes the confrontation of the two Latin authors more direct. (Petronius' life and works are the double object of imitation.) That Pushkin admired Tacitus' prose at this period we can infer from a remark of Aleksey Ivanych's in "Evening at the Dacha": "the dry and dull Aurelius Victor equals Tacitus in force of expression when he touches on Cleopatra." We cannot say for certain when Pushkin reread Tacitus, but the occasion seems to have brought into play associations over the range of Pushkin's acquaintance with the classics. In particular, the old connection Aurelius Victor-Tacitus revived from the sphere of interest of 1824, now bringing together Petronius and Cleopatra. The combination is unique to Pushkin, for Petronius' *Satyricon* does not include her.

For the first time in the Cleopatra cycle, but not the last, Pushkin has made the hero a poet; the poet and the hero of the times have become one. Petronius' last days pass in a villa whose owner loved the arts; statues of the nine Muses preside in the antechamber. His story is told to us by another poet, or at least poet-amateur, his young friend who contributes the anacreontic ode. What kind of poet is Petronius and what is the relation between the two poets, Petronius and his friend? Although "Egyptian Nights" also features a pair of poets, their relation seems quite different, at least as far as the fragment permits the comparison to go (see Chapter IV). In "A Tale from Roman Life," Pushkin makes a last attempt to incorporate into the pair the youth who possessed his imagination in the suggestive conclusion to the original Cleopatra poem, and whom Minsky had displaced. The historical Petronius as poet in and of society may have influenced Pushkin's later critical presentation of Charsky, but in "A Tale from Roman Life" we have Petronius' portrait only from the somewhat naive point of view of the young friend and enthusiast: "I respected his broad mind; I loved his beautiful soul." Their relation is somewhat reminiscent of that between Silvio and his young admirer in "The Shot." It is easy to be charmed by the tone of admiration and to make Petronius into something of an ideal poet. In fact, Pushkin is as interested in characterizing the youth through his remarks about Petronius. The two friends are counterweights. Petronius is distanced; and the naivete, the evident confusion and the sadness of this youth inspire in the reader the sympathy reserved for the young man who was Cleopatra's third lover. The first-person narration makes "A Tale from Roman Life" the youth's story, and the events of Petronius's last nights are played out for his benefit. He becomes the narrator while Petronius remains the story-teller (*razgovorshchik*). A hierarchy is implied which makes his story of a higher order than Petronius' several stories. There are autobiographical traits in Pushkin's Petronius, as in Charsky later, but this does not entitle us to assume that the stories are weighted in favor of the "Pushkin-hero."

Where Petronius rises in the reader's estimation is not in the youth's praise, but in the exchange of poems which takes place between the two on the subject of death. The youth, in the garden, on the bench—in the sentimental attitude—to assuage his sadness writes the equivalent of an elegy in the anacreontic ode. Youth *will* take the theme of death and age. "My hair is thin and gray" is pathos coming from him, instead of the love song which ought by rights to have occupied him and with which Petronius hails him, "You can tell a fiery steed." Although the youth may only be responding to the atmosphere of impending doom in the house, his attitude revives a mood from Pushkin's own early verse, the premature melancholy and fading away that followed on the "epicurean" beginnings. Petronius questions not his young friend's sincerity but Anacreon's. Anacreon's supposed fear of death is a false lead, like Horace's supposed cowardice in the ode which Petronius soon cites. Petronius' courage in surmounting the compromising circumstances of his situation by choosing death goes beyond the youth's comprehension. In this brief fragment Pushkin approaches a portentous subject, the death of the poet. In Akhmatova's words, he conceives it as "the voluntary departure from life of a strong man for whom to remain would be tantamount to losing his self-respect."[21]

The moral theme of the story, the courage to die, has just been defined in a dialogue between two poets. The sense of this private understanding is retained in "Egyptian Nights," where the collaboration of two poets produces the Cleopatra theme, although the character of the participants in the poetic exchange shifts. Pushkin leaves no doubt that these questions are the poets' province, that the poets are the best philosophers of ethics. To the youth who knows the world "more through the philosophy of the divine Plato than through his own experience," Petronius' freedom from philosophical party makes him the more attractive. "Indifference to everything spared him from prejudice," and, as a variant continued, "laziness from the errors of philosophy." In the plan, the "Greek philosopher" disappears from the feast: "The first night. We were so and so, the Greek philosopher disappears—Petronius smiles—and declaims an ode" (VI, 801). The "general conversation" of "Guests" 1830 has become in terms of the ancients a poetic symposium.

It returns us to the grouping of lovers at Cleopatra's feast in the 1824/28 poem with their characteristic, if somewhat conventionalized, "anacreontic," "epicurean," or "stoic" attitudes which are inadequate to define the youth upon whom Cleopatra rests her gaze. Two anthology lyrics, Pushkin's "Imitations of the Classics" of 1832 and two other poems of 1832-33, "The jolly god of the grape" and "Wine," are actually taken from the anthology of Atheneus entitled

The Feast of the Sophists via a French translation, Lefèvre's *Banquet des savants par Athénée*.[22] There is no reason to associate the feast particularly with Plato's *Symposium*—although the conjunction of the feast with the death of Petronius might suggest a conflation of the *Symposium* (whose theme is love and immortality) with scenes of Socrates' citizen's death in which the "corrupter of the youth of Athens" cheerfully drinks the hemlock, surrounded by friends who urge him to escape. The young friend in "A Tale from Roman Life" is a guest at this feast for which Petronius, his mentor, acts as master of the revels, as Cleopatra does for her feast. However, the youth himself is a poet and the situation—the two poets at the feast, one young and one old—is reminiscent of a plan of 1828, "The Poets' Feast":

> Youth: Leader of the feast, to you the first cup, etc.
> Old Poet: Thanks for your spirit—you honor my years, not my genius, that is extinguished.
> Youth: We honor your fame.
> Old Poet: What is fame? I enjoyed it, but it passed. Other times, other inspirations, another poet.
> The First: Sing us something.
> Old Poet: What shall I sing you?

(III, 496)

Whatever meaning this may have held in 1828 (Pushkin's dwindling popularity, his search for inspiration in other than "romantic" subjects, the "I need other scenes" of 1829, Onegin's journey), for 1833, "other times, other inspirations, another poet," perfectly expresses the predicament of Petronius, the "old poet" who would gladly be superseded.

Why did Pushkin reject the rich stylization of "A Roman Tale" for the contemporary voice in works written later in 1835? All explanations of the fact are hypothetical, but the chief effect was to retreat to a more neutral territory. Stylization might have *seemed* safer—all this is "then" and not now. But, paradoxically, even stylization was too direct, for the ancient world was accustomed to frankness. Politics, morality and religion—not irrelevant categories for the appreciation of the later fragments—were too clearly involved. Politics obtruded in the choice of Nero's reign, the omnipresence of the word "slave," the allegory of the "storm," the reference to exile and return from exile ("Which of the gods has restored to me"). Petronius' death is a form of civic action, a protest through acquiescence which expresses his solidarity with the courageous and sincere Horace who wrote, "*Dulce et decorum est pro patria mori.*" This exclamation is followed by a line of significant suspension points. Morality would be offended at the Cleopatra story which, in the apologetic words of "Evening at the Dacha," is "indecent like almost everything which vividly depicts the dreadful mores of antiquity." Religion would be outraged by the pagan end of the hero Petronius who proposes the mortal sin of suicide as a noble deed. The prospect of state, society and church censors in full and united cry may have contributed to turn Pushkin in the direction of parody rather than stylization.

This does not mean that the various censors would have had cause for complaint, that they would understand the deeper spirit of Pushkin's conception which was to fix on a moment of historical transition, the end of antiquity, and therefore the beginning of a new era. Petronius demonstrates courage, one of the cardinal virtues for the ancients. Plato wrote that the true philosopher makes a profession of dying (*Phaedo*, 67e) and Aristotle put courage first among the moral virtues in the *Nicomachean Ethics* (Bk. III, chs. 6-9). Pushkin understood that the Cleopatra anecdote had a characteristic appeal for the Roman Petronius. Where the tale of Antony and Cleopatra was concerned, even Octavian's propagandists were struck by Cleopatra's suicide, by her "Roman" death. In Horace's Cleopatra Ode (XXVII, Book I) "*Nunc est bibendum,*" the poet calls a feast to celebrate Cleopatra's downfall but ends with admiration for the courage of this proud queen to die, "*non humilis mulier.*" The battle of Actium is evoked in Propertius' elegy (VI, Book IV) where the poet concludes like Horace, but without Horace's generosity, "this only did she win, death at the hour of her own choice" ("*hoc unum, iusso non moritura die*"). Petronius uses a Cleopatra story to justify his own suicide. Historically, Aurelius Victor, whose anecdote was consistently Pushkin's foundation, was a contemporary of Julian the Apostate and sustained a high moral tone although in a Stoic rather than a Christian vein.[23] Pushkin had every reason to make "Cleopatra" part of a story of the Roman decadence.

Yet without concurring with Zhukovsky's praise of Pushkin as an exemplary Christian, we can read attentively, as Annenkov did, the end of the plan for "A Tale from Roman Life": "reflections on the fall of man—on the general lack of faith—on the superstitions of Nero—(Chr.) a Christian slave..." The intrusion of this Christian slave into the pagan symposium is very suggestive. Similar scenarios underlay manifest Christian pleading in Chateaubriand's *Les Martyrs*, in Thomas Moore, and later in Anatole France's *Thaïs*. The plan mentions lack of faith, *bezverie*, as a concomitant of the "fall"— a word which in itself suggests the Christian drama of salvation. The "Egyptian" society of "Guests" 1830 was nihilistic, believed in nothing. The poet, like a Christian in a secular society, is an anomaly, for he *believes*—in the reality of the passions, of history, of genius, of the moral powers. Whether or not Pushkin was religious, he looked on the ethical values of Christianity and its historico-philosophical role as progressive.

The stylization which he achieves in "A Tale from Roman Life" was not just a protective screen, therefore, but an indicator of the story's "otherness" and of the alien nature of the values to be found there. The decision of fate to grant a new life which Pushkin's heroes seek beginning with the late 1820's depends on which of two sets of values prevails: in the *Journey to Arzrum* the ark is moored to Mount Ararat "in the hope of renewal and life" while the raven and the dove fly out of it as "symbols of doom and reconciliation" (*kazn'* and *primirenie*) (VI, 670). In *The Captain's Daughter* Masha Mironova sues the Empress Catherine "not for justice but for mercy." Peter the Great uses his feast to pardon; the poet of "The Monument" will be remembered for seeking mercy for the fallen. All these works from the end of Pushkin's life celebrate mercy, a quality possible, no doubt, to the modern unbeliever but whose primacy in the hierarchy of values derives from Christian ethics. This is tantamount to a repeated attempt to motivate what Tomashevsky called the "psychological paradox" of Cleopatra's softened emotion in the poem of 1824. Already in *The Fountain of Bakhchisaray* the cross and the crescent matched the different faiths of the two heroines, and it was the gentle Maria who haunted Girey. It would be foolish to ignore the religious themes of the *Journey to Arzrum*, the documents of the Christian mission which Pushkin made its appendix, the unfinished narrative "Tazit" (which he began on his return) with its hero, the outcast Christian son of a warlike tribe. "Tazit" dates to 1829/30, according to the ten-volume edition which corrects without explanation older editions that referred to a second episode of work on the poem in 1833. "Tazit" grew out of an episode in the *Journey to Arzrum*, and most probably forms a link between that work and "A Tale from Roman Life." In both stories the "about to be Christian" youths are surrounded by their respective pagan societies.

Petronius with his Cleopatra story provides an example of the courage to die, of integrity in submission to judgment or nemesis, but not of the strength to live. The witness of his death who lived to tell of it was to have been the young poet-friend. Like the youth in the original Cleopatra poem he contributes an influx of sentiment as distinct from passion. Petronius carries out his decision without emotion; the youth grieves *for* him. In "Cleopatra" of 1824 the youth was a transformation of Pushkin's memory of himself as the vulnerable adolescent; by 1835 the youth is also associated with others like him who represent posterity, the spirit of the future. We remember the famous lines: "Whether I wander down noisy streets, or enter a crowded church, or sit among mad youth.... And let young life play at the door of the tomb"; "Hail, young and unknown race!" Two classicizing athlete statues, the subject of Pushkin's hexameters in 1836, represent Russian youths: "a youth full of beauty," "the youth took three strides" (III, 377). In Pushkin's adaptation of Bunyan, "The Wanderer" of 1835, the distraught hero meets the Evangelist, a "youth reading a book," who shows him the way. So in the context of late Pushkin Petronius' young friend belongs with the future and its values, the posterity which succeeded to antiquity. Decadence, broadly understood, is not just a decline and fall, but a time of transition and break with the past. Petronius as a hero of his time, of the Decadence, is like the modern hero: as readers of ancient history must all remark, modernity has happened twice. Indeed, crises of faith in politics and religion are constant companions of the end of any "old régime."

One of the alternative themes to "Cleopatra" in "Egyptian Nights" will be "The Last Day of Pompeii," the classic example of the end of a civilization. In 1834, between the beginning of his Roman tale and "Egyptian Nights," Pushkin wrote the fragment "Vesuvius opened its maw," whose semantics hint at political revolution as the elemental calamity which drives the people from their city. Pushkin was inspired by Bryullov's sensational historical canvas of "The Last Day." It is interesting to compare the composition of this heavily literary painting with Pushkin's plan for "A Tale from Roman Life": Bryullov illustrates the destruction of the old Roman world, symbolized by a chariot with broken axle reeling out of control and idols crashing from rooftops. The picture highlights, among others, a priest of the old order, a lone Christian and an artist modeled on the painter himself.[24]

Pushkin's attention was drawn to the analogy from antiquity

along with other analogies—the Puritan Revolution in England, the French Revolution with its religion of reason. The sumptuous villa and the feast of cosmopolitan philosophies in Pushkin's story of Petronius derive from his picture of the eighteenth century in "To a Grandee,"[25] the classicizing eighteenth century, an age which is ending in the poem, past in fact.

> At your austere feast
> Now reverencer of Providence, now sceptic, now atheist,
> Diderot would sit him down on his shaky tripod,
> Doff his wig, close his eyes in rapture
> And preach. And humbly you listened,
> Slowly sipping your glass, to atheist or deist,
> Like a curious Scythian to the Athenian Sophist.
> ....
> Crossing your threshhold,
> I am suddenly transported to the days of Catherine.
> The library, the statues and the paintings,
> And the graceful gardens testify to me
> That you are propitious to the Muses in tranquillity.
> ....
> Taking no part in the agitations of the world
> You sometimes gaze mockingly at them out the window
> And see in everything a cyclical turning.

> Thus, forgetting the whirlwind of affairs for the Muses and idle pleasure,
> In the retreat of porphyry baths and marble chambers
> Roman magnates once met their decline.
> And from afar, now a warrior, now an orator,
> Now a young consul, now a gloomy dictator,
> Would appear to rest a day or two in luxury,
> Sigh for a haven and set out once more upon his way.

(III, 169-71)

Pushkin informs us that this poem, too, belongs with the works which followed the journey to Arzrum: "On my return from Arzrum, I wrote the epistle to Prince Yusupov" (VII, 182). We note the presence of the restless guests in this splendid house who sigh for a haven and once more set off on their way. The poet numbers among them. No matter how beautiful the old "house of life," it is not home. Late antiquity, like the sunset years of the eighteenth century, is only a halting place in the extended poetic journey. The "Tale from

Roman Life" began: "Caesar was traveling... We reached Cumae and were thinking of going farther when... " (VI, 610). The ultimate destination lay beyond the bounds of that plot.

Probably one of the best-hidden classical quotations in Pushkin is a variation on the dictum *"tempora mutantur et nos mutamur in illis"*: *"Begut meniaias' nashi leta, meniaia vse, meniaia nas"* (III, 278; 1834); *"Proshli goda chredoiu nezametnoi, i kak oni peremenili nas"* (III, 174; 1836). What applies to a single lifetime is the more true of many generations. The aim of historical stylization is faithfully to reproduce not only the appearances of things and the manners of another time but also its habits of mind. These can be understood by analogy to our own but are ultimately alien. Perhaps Pushkin finally rejected homogeneous historical stylization in 1835 because it offered less scope for contrast in the treatment of a theme which required it, of a "psychological paradox." The youth planted in the midst and the Christian slave were not very convenient balancers. Pushkin had written: "The greatest spiritual and political revolution of our planet has been Christianity." In the Russian/Egyptian or Russian/Roman society it may seem as if Christianity had been in vain, almost as if it had never existed. Still, the modern sensibility had been changed by it. It is not only the censor who finds offense in the "dreadful mores of antiquity." Here is Pushkin's tentative answer in late 1836 to urgings that he be the one to translate Juvenal's Tenth Satire, a task which he began and abandoned almost immediately:

> One who prizes the colossal works of the mind,
> Friend of the English bards, lover of the Latin Muses,
> You again beckon me toward powerful antiquity,
> Again you bid me....
> Taking leave... of the dream and the poor ideal,
> I readied myself to contend with Juvenal,
> Whose stern verse, novice that I am,
> I had vowed to translate in verse, it seems.
> But, on opening these severe creations
> I could not overcome a timid embarassment...
> Shameless verses stick up like Priapus,
> Their sound is an ear-splitting strange harmony,
> Pictures... of Roman debauchery...[26]

(III, 380)

Pushkin as Juvenal, Pushkin as Petronius, Pushkin as satirist and only satirist, regrets the "dream" and the "poor ideal."

"Evening at the Dacha": The Alternative of Parody

The perspective in "Evening at the Dacha" is reversed: it looks back at antiquity from the present, not forward to a new era from the past. In this respect it is perhaps *a priori* a more pessimistic work than "A Tale from Roman Life." Yet the new story is based not on the certainty that history will repeat itself, but rather on the question of whether it will or not:

> —You should hand on this subject to Marquise George Sand, the same kind of a shameless hussy as your Cleopatra. She would adapt your Egyptian anecdote to today's mores.
> —Impossible. There would be no verismilitude. This anecdote is entirely classical; such a bargain is as impossible to bring about today as the construction of the pyramids.
> —How so, impossible to bring about?...
> —Let's say, that would be interesting to find out.

(VI, 606-07)

As Annenkov put it, Pushkin intended to draw from the probable difference "a strong romantic effect."[27]

Pushkin transmuted much of "A Tale from Roman Life" into "Evening at the Dacha."[28] The Cleopatra theme was again restored to plot value, no longer limited to a topic of philosophical conversation and touchstone of the good death as the ancients understood it. The dream of "happiness" and "bliss"—the love of Cleopatra's nights—again moved to the center. "Is life really such a treasure that I should mind buying happiness at the price of it... and will I be a coward when my bliss is at stake?" The Roman villa changed back again into a dacha, the story-telling figure and the motif of suicide (execution) entered the characterization of Aleksey Ivanych. The courageous suicide was assimilated to society mores via the custom of the duel and the honor of a gentleman. All is reduced to the private sphere; there can be no question of civic sentiments or of the political censor. The psychological and historical themes of satiety and decadence were channelled into the third Cleopatra poem. In the figure of Aleksey Ivanych, Pushkin retreated a little from the poet-hero, and the "we" of "we were spending the evening at the dacha" is a collective "we" of social observation, not the "*my s Titom Petroniem,*" the "we" of Petronius and the youth. The youth's separate viewpoint is absorbed into the ideological framework of the dual time-frame.[29] At the same time we can say that Pushkin took up "Guests" again after the attempt at classical stylization. He carried "Evening at the Dacha" as far as a tacit agreement between Volskaya, a name from the roster of "Guests," and Aleksey Ivanych, Minsky's literary cousin. Volskaya raises and lowers her "fiery" or "fiery and penetrating" eyes every time that Aleksey Ivanych touches on Cleopatra's demand ("*uslovie Kleopatry*")—she has the Cleopatra glance. For Akhmatova she was the demonic woman of whom Pushkin decided "yes, she would be capable of it," fearsome yet fatally alluring.[30]

Another familiar signal from "Guests" is "conversation." In fact, "Evening at the Dacha" falls into two sections, one beginning "the conversation somehow touched on Mme de Staël," the other, "the conversation changed." The first introduces a frame dialogue, the anecdote about Madame de Staël and Napoleon, leading into Aleksey Ivanych's performance as the "conversationalist," the Cleopatra poem. The second introduces Aleksey Ivanych's private exchange with Volskaya, a new element, expressed as the "change of conversation."[31] Madame de Staël, implicit in the background of "Guests" 1830, is used explicitly to launch the old theme of genius and heroes into the flagging conversational gambit of Saint Petersburg. Her anecdote as told by a guest is naturally distorted into an amusing epigram and elicits the characteristic remark from the spectator on the sidelines: "You do not believe in the Genius' simplicity of spirit." Madame de Staël had asked Napoleon whom he considered "the foremost woman in the world," to which he replied, "she who has had the most children." We might have expected the new Caesar to have proposed Cleopatra, but true to his imperial character, Napoleon prefers woman as the begetter of new armies rather than their leader. He is the Roman consolidator of revolution, the family man. This is reminiscent of the "quarrel between the brunette and the blond" in the plan for "Guests" 1828, especially when Aleksey Ivanych proposes Cleopatra. The guests' suggestions (whether right-thinking royalist or salon-radical revolutionary—Madame de Staël, Joan of Arc, Elizabeth of England, Madame de Maintenon, Madame de Roland) are sandwiched between the only two ideas with any force of imagination, Napoleon's and Aleksey Ivanych's.

This conversation takes place at the dacha during the evening: we are in the atmosphere of the Egyptian nights. Aleksey Ivanych's Cleopatra anecdote, "your Egyptian anecdote," is prepared by the episodic character Soloukhin who speaks of the "Genius' simplicity of spirit," only just rousing from the somnolence into which the company has evidently plunged him. "Soloukhin, drowsing in the Rameses armchair...the guests began to argue and Soloukhin dozed off again." We are also in the familiar frozen desert of society: Aleksey Ivanych, unable to warm to the conversation, warms himself at the fire. He is the "young man standing by the fireplace, because in Petersburg a fireplace is never superfluous." Of course, he is attracted by the fire in the eyes of Volskaya. The wider conversation still continues to take a satirical direction. "Evening at the Dacha" gathers elements from both "Guests" and "A Tale from Roman Life." Perhaps "Egyptian Nights" would have maintained the momentum and incorporated the new plot development of "Evening at the Dacha." A drawing-room discussion might have followed the improvisor's performance, for instance.

Pushkin has returned to the society tale, but with a difference— the bodily intrusion of the Cleopatra poem. The poems are no longer only "buried." Literature is one of the topics of society talk, such as it is, centering on the relation of the ancients and the moderns and of art to life. The whole plot of the story revolves around a parody, a creative reworking of literary material and of history itself. Here, as in *Count Nulin*, Pushkin intended to parody both.

We may ask how the idea to parody this particular material arose. The schematism deliberately adopted in the character portraiture is peculiar, the lack of psychological biographies, the exaggerated physical gestures—fiery eyes, breaking voice. Akhmatova suspected that Aleksey Ivanych's "heavy, almost translated prose" had been lifted from a French romantic novel.[32] This may well have been Janin's *Barnave*, as Lednicki argues.[33] Pushkin read the book in 1831 and expressed the desire to write an article about its author. The comparison is tempting: similar use of a contemporary frame story with anecdotes (a composition which suggests correspondences), similar problematics of decadence, indeed, one episode that features Cleopatra in a "half-poetical, half-erotic" account, and another in which the internal narrator presents himself as almost the incarnation of a notorious and lascivious Roman. Ideologically, as Vatsuro put it, "the era of Cleopatra and the Alexandrian kingdom was explored as a historical analogue to the era of 1789 in France."[34] Pushkin must have been attracted by the interpenetration of the exotic and the ordinary in Janin's novel, the stylistic variety, the ambiguous tone. Lednicki is right that despite the excesses of the *école frénetique* its expressive situations and stark contrasts interested Pushkin.[35] Perhaps in "Evening at the Dacha" Pushkin is even gratifying the desire of Janin's narrator to visit Russia with its scandalous history.[36]

However, the Cleopatra story which appears in *Barnave* is not Pushkin's distinctive plot based on Aurelius Victor, and, more importantly, Janin's work was one of the "new novels" whose pathos Pushkin presents as in reality inadequate to the ancient anecdote. Janin's *Barnave* takes its place as one of a variety of models which fed Pushkin's interest in parody, strikingly witnessed already in 1829 by Liza in "A Novel in Letters":

> An intelligent person could take a ready-made plan, ready-made characters, correct the style and absurdities, make up the omissions— and a splendid original novel would result. Tell this to my ungrateful P. from me... Let him embroider new patterns on the old canvas and present to us in a small frame a picture of the society and people that he knows so well.

(VI, 67)

If "Evening at the Dacha" is a parody or reworking of Janin and not simply an imitation of him, it is safe to say that his "style, absurdities and omissions" did not escape correction.

In the terminology of the society genres the Cleopatra story becomes "*vash egipetskii anekdot*" (J. VIII₂, 985). What the society audience calls *anekdot*, Aleksey Ivanych refers to as *skazanie*; where they see the makings of an obscene joke (*anekdot*), he envisions a whole narrative poem (*poèma*). *Anekdot* is already slightly pejorative here: the society audience will be entertained by the "conversationalist" while the readers of the story have also to penetrate the meaning of the author.[37] Janin helps us with the "conversationalist," but it would be dangerous to identify him with the author. The guests suggest that material comparable to the Cleopatra story exists among the contemporary romantics. Aleksey Ivanych understands Cleopatra to be motivated not by love but rather by an abandoned imagination (*pylkost' voobrazheniia*). The guests put forward Dumas' *Antony*, Balzac's *Physiologie du mariage*, and George Sand. "That is nothing compared to the new novels" (variant, J. VIII₂, 991). A variant of the fair copy even named *Barnave*. Yet the implication is that whatever the romantics touch, they paint only themselves and their own age: "George Sand... she would have expressed herself" (J. VIII₂, 985). Pushkin agreed and

93

often deplored the exclusively French influence on Russian literary taste. The guests' comparisons show us only the point of departure. We can safely assume that there never *has* been anything so shocking as the Cleopatra anecdote. For all their bluffing, the ladies are horrified, horrified and puzzled—"How awful! the ladies objected. What do you find so amazing about it?" The new novels do not really understand the true romanticism. What Pushkin wants to bring home is a kind of literalism, a simplicity, a life and death directness to the Cleopatra anecdote. This desire illuminates the deeper function of the apparently "descriptive" or "historical" stylization in the third "Cleopatra" and "A Tale from Roman Life." "Evening at the Dacha" insists: "Napoleon literally expressed his opinion. But you do not believe in the Genius' simplicity of spirit" (VI, 601); "Tell me simply what you know about Cleopatra…" (VI, 603). Cleopatra is a woman who challenged men to take literally the romantic cliché, "I love you better than my life." The story is "realist" in that it tends to prove the reality of all the things engulfed by the nihilism of the "Egyptian" society; passion is real, genius is real, history, too, is real.

A passage marked in Pushkin's copy of Hazlitt's celebrated essay, "On the Fear of Death," and which seems to have escaped critical notice, strikingly summarizes the point of view represented in "Evening at the Dacha":

> The effeminate clinging to life as such, as a general or abstract idea, is the effect of a highly civilized and artificial state of society. Men formerly plunged into all the vicissitudes and dangers of war, or staked their all upon a single die, or some one passion, which if they could not have gratified, life became a burthen to them—now our strongest passion is to think, our chief amusement is to read new plays, new poems, new novels, and this we may do at our leisure, in perfect security, *ad infinitum*. If we look into the old histories and romances, before the *belles-lettres* neutralised human affairs and reduced passion to a state of mental equivocation, we find the heroes and heroines not setting their lives "at a pin's fee," but rather courting opportunities of throwing them away in very wantonness of spirit. They raise their fondness for some favourite pursuit to its height, to a pitch of madness, and think no price too dear to pay for its full gratification. Everything else is dross. They go to death as to a bridal bed, and sacrifice themselves or others without remorse at the shrine of love, of honor, religion, or any other prevailing feeling.[38]

Hazlitt's phrase about "the old histories and romances, before the *belles-lettres* neutralised human affairs" is particularly telling in the context of "Evening at the Dacha." Here, as in "Egyptian Nights," the ancient literary anecdote is potent, quite the opposite of the neutralizing modern *belles-lettres*. The poem about Cleopatra acts to stir Aleksey Ivanych and Volskaya; the poet-friend has moved them with his art; they seem locked into ancient history and into the anecdote.

But this is still too simple. For Pushkin, the strength of romantic identification was also its weakness. We have still the *question* of repetition; the outcome of the story is in doubt.[39] In none of his parodic works is Pushkin interested in establishing a true repetition; on the contrary, the nature of the deviation from the expected is what the reader is left to discover. "Evening at the Dacha" might be different, of course. There are three theoretically pure possibilities— tragedy, farce and comedy. Tragedy if the repetition is perfect; farce ("tragedy the second time around") if the repetition is imperfect; comedy (the happy ending) if the repetition is eluded altogether. But Madame de Staël held that tragedy was an impossibility in modern high society,[40] and Tomashevsky thought that the appreciation of uniqueness and change precluded repetition pure and simple.[41] Next to historicism, aestheticism is the other limiting force: how far will Pushkin allow the characters to be possessed by the Cleopatra poem? Let us take a somewhat comparable case, the anecdote of the three cards in "The Queen of Spades." There, Herman is convinced, hypnotized by the account which he hears of the way to attain fortune (*shchastie*—like the happiness and bliss of "Evening at the Dacha"). "It was a joke," says the old Countess. Herman is unable at last to make the past yield up its secret, and the garbled version of the answer he seeks when prompted by his own desires leads him to disaster. He is not even liberated from the power of the anecdote by his failure—even in his madness it obsesses him. In "The Queen of Spades" and in "Evening at the Dacha" the anecdotes are in the nature of grandiose temptations for the pseudo-Napoleonic hero.

Characteristically, the onus of temptation has been shifted away from the Cleopatra. She remains the temptress of the actual poem, naturally, in Aleksey Ivanych's imagination. But in the contemporary story it is Aleksey Ivanych who suggested the theme to his poet-friend, and it is the poet's version which he uses to appeal to Volskaya. Aleksey Ivanych approaches *her* with this poetic fiction, not she him. This is the way that it happens in the modern age. It is hard to escape the conclusion that the ancient anecdote has been debased. Ultimately, Pushkin's management of the literary parody depends on the slant that he gives to his parody of history, that is, on his assessment of modernity, its losses and its gains.

A perspective of historical decadence shadows Pushkin in the 1830's. Take, for instance, *The Journey to Arzrum* and *The Bronze Horseman*. Pushkin notes with irony that Arzrum is captured on the anniversary of Poltava, and the whole journey goes to show that there are no more glories in nineteenth-century Russian imperial wars. In *The Bronze Horseman* the new tsar cannot command the forces of nature as Peter could, and Peter's stylized eighteenth-century ode must give way to the nineteenth-century tale. One of the themes of conversation in "A Tale from Roman Life" before Petronius dictates his *Satyricon* is given as "the fall of the gods, the fall of man." The 1835 "Cleopatra" puts a new emphasis on satiety in the psychology of its heroine; the setting is expressly Alexandrian. But what we might call the heroic decadence of the poem becomes a standard, perhaps a lost one, against which to test the tenor of the Petersburg tale which follows.

Stylization and parody are means of indirection, literary devices which divert attention away from the author. We must respect his desire for anonymity without disregarding the greater human problems around which he constructs his works. Akhmatova ventured to say that Pushkin had his esoteric writing ("*a tainopis'u Pushkina byla*").[42] She conjectured that he resorted to it when approaching the "agonizing nexus" of a persistent psychological complex: *tedium vitae*, the question of the value of existence, an intense love of life coupled with an equally great fear of attaining happiness, a superstitious dread of some terrible punishment. The writing has its roots in "an underlying level which poets almost hide from themselves."[43] Akhmatova concluded, "'All that doesn't sound very much like Pushkin,' they'll tell me.—No, not very much, not like the Pushkin we know, the author of *Eugene Onegin*; but we do not know him especially well even a bit later as the author of his *Diary*."[44] If to finish "Evening at the Dacha" would have meant deciding the case for or against modernity, to finish "Egyptian Nights" would also have meant deciding one's own fate as a poet joined to a man of the world with all his painful complexes. In "Egyptian Nights" the two are one character, and it is the fate of the artist that hangs suspended. We do not know late Pushkin very well if we do not recognize his need for "romantic" devices to develop such a theme.

IV

"EGYPTIAN NIGHTS": THE POETIC FUSION

In "Egyptian Nights," Pushkin thinks backward from the
Cleopatra poem, which, it must be remembered, had been
significantly recast for "Evening at the Dacha." The third and last
chapter of "Egyptian Nights" containing the Cleopatra improvisation is the end of the chain of development which led through
"Guests," "A Tale from Roman Life," and "Evening at the Dacha."
In "Egyptian Nights," two new chapters precede the Cleopatra
material; they climax in the first, private improvisation and introduce
the new hero, the poet, or rather the pair of poets. Thus, "Egyptian
Nights" contains an artist story. To some it is a piece of meta-
literature about the poet and the creative act. Matlaw called it
"Pushkin's last pronouncement on the poet and poetry."[1] The story
would seem to be about a distinction between two kinds of poet or
two roles within the poet. It also treats the poet and his relation to
society and seemingly translates into prose Pushkin's lyrics about his
calling, adapting them to real life.[2] It has been seen as Pushkin's
polemic against the romantic artist and the romantic artist story, one
of its aims being to discredit the myth of the improvisor as an
inspired, prophetic figure.[3] These interpretations tend to suffer from
a dogmatic attitude toward romanticism and its possible place in late
Pushkin. More importantly, they are too dry. The story was not
meant to be a literary-critical construct: "Egyptian Nights" has not
ceased to be a Cleopatra story. The most vexed problem in its
interpretation is the relation between the two parts, the story of the
poets on the one hand and that of Cleopatra on the other.[4]

The work is one, as we will show by relating its two poetic
improvisations along with their special prose introductions.
However, the place to begin is with the very nature of the
improvisations, the most striking device in the story. The
improvisations are perhaps a more natural way to motivate the
introduction of poetry into prose than Aleksey Ivanych's recitation
of his friend's work in "Evening at the Dacha." But they do far more
than satisfy the demands of verisimilitude. They represent a form of
indirect discourse through poetry at which Pushkin arrived by
literary necessity. In the history of the Cleopatra material as it

appears in Pushkin's prose settings, the improvisations stand in place of the previous polemical conversations bearing on the spiritual death or emptiness of the Russian society world.

From the perspective of the cycle as a whole, the significant shift witnessed there was one from conversation to poem. The various conversations of "Guests" are largely banished by poems from the symposium around which Pushkin constructed the first successor story "A Tale from Roman Life," the fragment with the poet Petronius as its hero. As we remember, its plan reads: "the Greek philosopher has disappeared—Petronius smiles—and declaims an ode" (VI, 801). In "Guests" we had buried poems, in "Egyptian Nights" we have disguised conversations. Both literally and figuratively there is an argument behind "Egyptian Nights." It may be said that the indirection of the story stems from an author's impasse: how is he to address important issues before a society which does not recognize his values? Pushkin has been forced to abandon the idea of explaining and thus trying to bridge the gap between society and his reflective heroes. He had hoped to further a "general conversation," an ideal discourse in which literature was one participant, society the other. This hope was repeatedly frustrated. The themes for the improvisations are materials for a performance, a spectacle on which society gazes. Retreating behind the improvisation, Pushkin said, in effect, "What do I mean? Let me tell you a story..." Two voices, indeed, enter into a conversation about art and about Cleopatra, but they are only the isolated voices of the two poets.

It is thus that the conversing heroes of the previous prose fragments become a pair of poets in "Egyptian Nights" and that the tale of Cleopatra takes on the added dimension of an artist story. The heroes of "Egyptian Nights"—Charsky and the Italian improvisor—have a double role to play. First, being artists they serve as public "conversationalists," to use the revealing term from the draft of "Guests." The social function created by Pushkin's jesting neologism is qualitatively different from the related ones of the *beau-parleur* or *raconteur*, the wit or retailer of anecdotes. These had an important literary cousin in the *conteur* or storyteller. The "conversationalist," social or literary, may hold forth in brilliant monologues, but only because he is striving to replace the dialogue which he cannot stimulate. However, in "Egyptian Nights" the poets are not just discussants, they are also actors and characters. In the conception of "Egyptian Nights" there remains the society tale of "Guests" and its progeny, except that "Egyptian Nights" has as its chief hero the poet

Charsky. His tragedy is that the man in him who doubles the poet must be a man of the world and thus is likely to be drawn into a repetition of the Cleopatra drama. But "Egyptian Nights" is a "Guests" in which the social stage has become a visible stage, and where the gypsy-like ticket-taker in attendance belongs more to artistic Bohemia than to any European nation.

It is the improvisations which have accomplished the poetic fusion. The new poet line is fruitfully grafted onto the old material, the story of Cleopatra and her lovers. The poets take part in both sides of the plot. They are analogues to Minsky—the man of the world who replaced the youth of the original Cleopatra poem as the favored lover—and also to Cleopatra herself. The second climactic improvisation, the burst of poetic speech in the face of Petersburg society, imitates Cleopatra's own declamation with equal effect: "She spoke, and horror gripped them, / Passion shuddered in their hearts."

So it makes sense to work back from the end as we have it, the scene containing the second improvisation. This is the decisive moment towards which the whole exposition has been moving. The Cleopatra story—lives bartered for a night of love—and the open question of its repetition in the present day remain at the core of "Egyptian Nights." The text contains no explicit expression of this, no exchange between a modern Cleopatra and her lover, unlike "Evening at the Dacha." Instead, allusion carries the meaning.

One set of underlying correspondences in the story has long been noted: the correspondence between the world of late antiquity and the decadent life of nineteenth-century Petersburg society, carried out artistically as a correspondence between motifs in the second poetic improvisation and motifs of its prose introduction.[5] The setting of the gala performance echoes the setting of the Cleopatra poem, the Petersburg atmosphere models the inertia of her Egyptian nights, the theatrical speech of the Italian improvisor doubles the speech of the Alexandrian queen. The self-possession of the regal young beauty who draws the Cleopatra theme marks her out as the potential heroine, the modern-day Cleopatra. However, there is another correspondence inherent in the structuring of the scene which actively binds the analogy. Two acts intimately connected with the Italian's improvisation, but deriving from the Cleopatra poem, also take on broad thematic significance: the challenge to the audience and the drawing of lots. They are, in effect, symbolic acts, the statements of a frustrated conversation between poet and society.

One more significant detail forms a final link between poem and prose: the porcelain vase which receives the themes for the improvisation and from which the Cleopatra theme is drawn. This is the double of the "fatal urn" which held the lots of Cleopatra's lovers.

Here, then, is the central passage; it takes us to the very source of the modern Cleopatra plot:

> —Having mounted his platform again, the improvisor placed the urn on the table and began to take the slips of paper from it one by one.
> —What does my honored public command? asked the humble Italian. Will they set me one of the themes I am offered for themselves or will they leave it to lots?
> —By lots!... spoke one voice from the crowd.
> —By lots, by lots!... the audience repeated.
>
> The improvisor again descended from the platform with the urn in his hands and asked, "Whom may it please to draw the theme?" The improvisor scanned the first rows of seats with an imploring look. Not one of the brilliant ladies seated there moved. The improvisor, who was unaccustomed to northern indifference, seemed to be suffering... suddenly he noticed a hand raised to the side in a little white glove; he turned round eagerly and approached a regal young beauty sitting on the end of the second row. She rose and without the least embarrassment and with all possible simplicity dropped her little aristocratic hand into the urn and drew out a slip of paper.
> —Be so good as to open it and read it, the improvisor said to her. The young beauty unfolded the paper and read aloud:
> —*Cleopatra e i suoi amanti.*

(VI, 384-85)

In poetic usage the urn is a symbol of destiny. It signals that contemporary Petersburg is approaching another moment of fate. The staging is significant. At the decisive moment an indifferent, northern society refuses to choose: "By lots, by lots!" the audience choruses. If, as Akhmatova was convinced, there was a moralist at work in Pushkin the artist,[6] it may be that the moment embodies poetic justice. Poetic justice here decrees, precisely because society will not choose, that it must *therefore* be the Cleopatra theme which emerges from the urn, a theme which confronts the audience imaginatively with the very same situation, a drama of choice and personal commitment. The moral torpor of society, a topic of earlier conversation, brings on the theme which means nemesis: it produces Cleopatra with her sentence of death.

Who is the unwitting instrument of this poetic justice? The poet himself. It has not been stressed enough that there is a studied ambiguity as to exactly who has proposed Cleopatra as a subject: perhaps the plain girl who wrote down a theme at the behest of her mother (this would make it the vicarious fantasy of the predatory matron or else of the not-so-innocent maiden). But when Charsky announces that the theme is his we may believe him. For he proceeds to clarify it so promptly and precisely that it is evident that Cleopatra has been the center of his own reflections. Pushkin writes of him: "Charsky was very concerned for the success of the performance... he had a feeling that the thing would not go forward without him" (VI, 382-84).

The theme of a fatal southern love for an inwardly rebellious poet has obvious personal significance. This might well be the belated revenge of the romantic, familiar from the society tale. Pushkin left suggestive testimony for a subjective application when he marked, in the whole of Madame de Staël's *Corinne*, just the pages concerning the fatal power of destiny over the poet isolated in the world, lines which form the climax of one of the heroine's grandiloquent improvisations:

> Thus talent, aghast at the desert which surrounds it, roams the universe without finding its like.... Common spirits take for madness this malaise of a soul which does not breathe enough air in this world, enough enthusiasm, enough hope.

> Fate, Corinne continued with ever-rising emotion, does not fate pursue elevated souls, poets whose imagination depends on their ability to love and suffer?... What did the ancients mean when they spoke of destiny with such terror? What power does it have, destiny, over common and placid spirits?[7]

Objectively speaking, however, it is no surprise that Charsky, as one of the "quintessential inhabitants" of Petersburg, should simply have his own particular understanding of a theme which belongs to his city at large, and that the poet who abhors society's claims on him, even while he lives as a man of the world, should be forced to explain to the public its intimate thoughts. Charsky interprets society's Cleopatra theme, transmitting it to the improvisor who takes it up and develops it. Both poets act as mediums.

Turn-of-the-century critics in the symbolist era devoted a great deal of energy to defining the "societal aspect," *moment obshchestvennosti,* in "Egyptian Nights."[8] The improvisation seemed the expression of the collectivity—a sort of theatrical priestly rite. The improvisor, like a leader communicating with the Greek dramatic chorus, represented the primal collective impulse toward poetic expression. He was opposed to Charsky, the creature of Pushkin as renegade, to the alienation of the modern, individualistic lyric consciousness.[9] The conflict is only apparent. Pushkin makes the two collaborate, and the story becomes a form of action in spite of alienation.

The urn of destiny is also a symbol of death. Yet the Cleopatra theme which emerges from it in "Egyptian Nights" does not indulge morbid sensationalism, because for the poet it comes as an imposed theme, even the result of a kind of social command, implicit in the cries of the society crowd. And, by means of it, he aims to effect the paradoxical poetic animation of the silent and impassive weight of the neo-Egyptian society. This animation is the motivation behind the improvisation. It springs from the Cleopatra poem itself: "The queen with voice and glance / Animated her luxurious feast." The dramatic moment in "Egyptian Nights" is the moment of choice; for choice, which has been regarded by some philosohers of our day as *the* human act, is the very principle of animation—in an older language, of the "movements of the soul." The improvisation contains an inspired appeal to the latent passions. It is the poet's challenge (as it was Cleopatra's), his attempt at moving the society with which he cannot converse. The Italian's discomfiture when surrounded by the profound silence of the hall is a dramatization of the predicament discussed in the conversations of "Guests": "The improvisor, who was unaccustomed to northern indifference, seemed to be suffering . . . " The essential is to waken some living action, but the pessimistic conditions of the story dictate that this shall only be a reaction to an event or happening in the sphere of art.

At this point it should be noted that the historical theme of "Egyptian Nights," that of the Decadence, is capable of political extension.[10] The 1828 conversation had political overtones. Even the 1824 Cleopatra poem may be viewed from this angle as the picture of an adulatory court before its autocratic idol in an atmosphere of mercenary corruption, of Asiatic splendor and inertia. The Cleopatra poem, as the new context of "Caesar" showed, could be a part of a modern poet's Satyricon. The impassive silence of Petersburg society in "Egyptian Nights" was a historical condition suggesting poetic analogies; it proceeded, of course, from political causes. The crucial moment which launches the Cleopatra theme is a moment of voidness which can be matched in dramatic import by the famous and enigmatic stage direction which ends *Boris Godunov*: "The people are silent." Referring the moment in Pushkin's work to the poet's situation: he is caught between the silent, inarticulate and perhaps hostile masses on the one hand, and the equally silent high society on the other. "Egyptian Nights" returns to the drama of the pretenders and the Russian silence.

Where a sense of history is absent, where the literature and politics which for Pushkin are the foundation for a genuine conversation do not exist, we can expect the intrusion of poetic fictions as mythological reality. As a result, however far-reaching its historical and political ramifications, "Egyptian Nights" draws its greatest effect from a psychology of suggestion which deliberately borders on the fantastical.[11]

With this background we can attempt to bridge the gap which seems to exist between the first two chapters of "Egyptian Nights" and the third chapter. Essentially, this means elaborating on the relation between the poets and Cleopatra. For some readers there is no necessary relation between them. However, Dostoevsky once explained of his characters as carriers of ideas that ideas do not exist in the abstract, that every idea belongs to someone. We have in "Egyptian Nights" not so much a story about Cleopatra or about the artist; rather we have a story about the Cleopatra idea as one belonging to the artist. This blended story is based on a series of assimilations. As one critic put it, Pushkin is less concerned with the "realization of dichotomies" than with the "fusion of contrasts."[12]

To begin with, the improvisor is clearly likened to Cleopatra, the principle being that the original Cleopatra was a sort of poet, the eloquent instigator of a plot full of romantic drama, and the poet, in turn, resembles her in his actions. As already noted, the improvisor varies Cleopatra's speech and her challenge. It is, of course, in the improvisor's moment as inspired romantic poet that he seems to mimic her, when, in the infernal black which recalls her oath by Hades, in the cross-armed stance of the man of fate, his high forehead bearing like hers the marks of thought, he takes the dramatic step forward to address his theme. Compare "She rises to meet them. / It is accomplished . . . " For Cleopatra and the crowd we substitute the poet and the crowd. This is nothing else but the subject of the first improvisation. The poet whose definition is framed by the epigraph from Derzhavin—"I am a king, a slave, a worm, a god"—

understands the queen who is both high and low, who can rise to sublimity even while debasing herself as a prostitute. By circumstances and by nature Cleopatra becomes the poet's theme. If we may judge by the fragment "We Spent the Evening at the Dacha" the poet is also the modern Cleopatra's lover.

The Cleopatra improvisation, a public event, has been foreshadowed by a preliminary improvisation, which represents the culmination of two new chapters, a private matter for the ears of poets only. Romantic works demanded literary prefaces, and Pushkin follows this practice in his presentation. What this means is that the inception of the Cleopatra plot had acquired a programmatic aesthetic value. Pushkin tells us as much if we look back to the note appended to the fragment of 1830 which was revised for the characterization of Charsky in Chapter I of "Egyptian Nights"— "This fragment probably formed the preface to a story not yet written or now lost."[13]

The first improvisation deals explicitly with the question of the social command. It contains a polemic against the idealists' elevated view of the poet, and it defends the treatment of so-called low subjects:[14]

"......
A trifling subject continually
Disturbs and allures you.
Genius should strive for the skies.
A true poet is obliged
To take an elevated subject
For his inspired songs."
—Why does the wind whirl in the gully,
Raise the leaves and sweep the dust,
While a ship on the still waters
Avidly awaits its breath?
Why does the eagle, heavy and fearsome,
Fly from the hills and past the towers
Onto a withered stump? Ask him.
Why does the young Desdemona
Love her Moor
As the moon loves the gloom of night?
Because there is no law
For wind, or eagle, or a maiden's heart.
Such is the poet: like the Aquilon
He sweeps along what he wishes—
Like the eagle, he flies,

And, asking leave of no one,
Like Desdemona he chooses
The idol of his heart.

(VI, 379-80)

Yet this passage cuts two ways. If it is an apology for realism, then this is realism of the romantic sort, based on radical freedom from convention and from "laws." The first improvisation is more than a brilliant theoretical digression. Pushkin is here preparing his poet for the Cleopatra theme. The low is demonstratively, romantically, low; yet the impulse which the poet retains is high, even when directed at low objects. The social command in the first improvisation was that the poet should take elevated themes. In Chapter I, Charsky is described as chafing under the public's narrow understanding of "poetic liberties," and he is hardly able to refrain from some act of provocative rudeness or crudity (*grubost'*). It would seem that his hand is itching to deliver some slap in the face of public taste. The Cleopatra theme as interpreted by the pair of poets represents the meeting of the elevated moment of poetic inspiration with its "low" object, a synthesis arrived at here in the first improvisation.

We now return to the series of assimilations which blend the two lines of the story. The Italian improvisor has been compared to Cleopatra. Next he is to be related to Charsky. Much has been written of their opposition. But Pushkin contrasts them the better to highlight their similarities. The two are paired; in some ways they are even doubles. The Cleopatra improvisation can be viewed as their common creation. This is certainly true of the first improvisation: there the improvisor spontaneously develops Charsky's protest against the social command. In that each is a true poet, they are alike, different as their social positions may be. And the improvisor is a vivid and unpleasant reminder to the haughty Charsky of the poet's dependence on a society which he despises. They share the divided nature and the double life of the poet who is now man, now artist, of the poet who is being prepared for the Cleopatra theme. The first two chapters are organized around the appearance of the Italian, under rather remarkable circumstances, and his eventual full but reluctant recognition by Charsky. Again, as in Chapter III and the action of the Cleopatra improvisation, there is a drama to these psychological events which has fantastical overtones.

The appearance of the Italian to Charsky can deservedly be called a psychological event, for he arrives on the heels of Charsky's fit of inspiration. The structuring of this sequence makes him materialize on the scene out of Charsky's imagination. After the characterization of Charsky's life in society, when the inner and poetical side of it begins to be illustrated, at a moment of heightened perception and released expression, the stranger crosses the threshold of Charsky's room. A Freudian might say that a repressed image of the self, having circumvented the societal censor, seems to have thrust its way into consciousness, demanding to be recognized and integrated. In Pushkin's text this is done by means of allusions to the end of the poem "Autumn": Charsky has reached the state "when verses fall lightly under your pen and resonant rhymes run to meet harmonious thoughts." Several critics have noticed this resemblance without recalling that it leads up to the open end of "Autumn," to the potential point of insertion for stanzas which, in the manuscript continuation, had brought back the creatures of Pushkin's young romantic imagination. The Italian is thus like one of the famous "swarm of guests" (from the final text) who join the poet, the "old acquaintances and fruits of his fancy." The moment when the Italian appears matches the action of the improvisation in Chapter III—a moment of magical animation when fictions come to life. The improvisor's introduction stresses this: Charsky is in a state "when dreams clearly take shape before you," "living, unexpected words for the incarnation of your visions." The stranger is really a familiar, a kind of alter ego. He arrives with inspiration and has a sure instinct for developing Charsky's poetic themes as if they were his own. Of course there will be no conflict between inner and outer, between inspiration and the will of others, a conflict which Charsky assumes to exist. It is the coincidence between the two elements that sets up the mysterious vibrations in Chapter III. There, the poets' chosen theme and the theme which falls to society by lot are indeed one and the same. The new chapters represent a private rehearsal for the public performance.

Charsky proposes to the Italian a theme which requires him to criticize the social command: "The poet himself chooses the subjects of his songs. The crowd has no right to direct his inspiration." In so doing, Charsky issues a challenge and even deals a personal insult, since the improvisor's livelihood depends on his response to the "will of others." This would seem to be a well-nigh impossible theme for the Italian, and to suggest it betrays a certain hostility on Charsky's part. However, by the end of the duel of wits Charsky is completely won over, disarmed. At the end of Chapter II the seemingly implausible reciprocal bond between Charsky and the Italian is completed. A final passage refers back internally to the moment in Chapter I when the foreigner appeared. The swiftness of impressions and thoughts emerging already armed with four rhymes to which the improvisor alludes at the end compare with the reminiscences from "Autumn" which describe Charsky's inspiration. Thus, the Italian is foreign and yet not alien. If Charsky is akin to the improvisor and the improvisor, in turn, to Cleopatra, then the artistic syllogism closes upon Charsky and Cleopatra. The Petersburg poet is matched with the Egyptian queen against Petersburg society. "Egyptian Nights" is a work with a dynamic action in which poets are movers and where associative devices, ranging from the chain of assimilations just discussed through historical correspondences, compensate for the state of dissociation prevailing in the story (the isolation of the poet and the atomization of society).

It may be objected that this reading of "Egyptian Nights" depends on taking the improvisor more seriously than is usually done. He might seem to be the weak link in the chain. Certain aspects of the consensus of interpretation mitigate against him, and these deserve to be re-examined. With Pushkin the divided nature of the poet, now man, now artist, casts no reproach on art. Let the poet be the most ordinary of men, the fire of inspiration only becomes the more mysterious. It goes without saying that the improvisor is not discredited as an artist by human foibles like avarice and obsequious deference to his betters. Pushkin summed up his potential social roles thus: "meeting this man in the woods you would have taken him for a robber; in society—for a political conspirator; in the ante-chamber— for a charlatan trafficking in elixirs and arsenic" (VI, 374). However disreputable he may be in life (perhaps even sympathetically so for the non-conformist), on stage he is a king. The improvisor need not be an ideal figure by any means. However, he has obvious poetic power, and he alone is left to disprove what sounds very much like a maxim of the spiritually dead Petersburg society on the lips of Charsky—"The calling of the poet does not exist with us."

Such negative statements representing a denial of values were consistently used to characterize the society viewpoint in various fragments of "Guests" where, in fact, the society tale was the predominant genre aspect. "Passions! What a big word! What are passions?" (VI, 562). Variant: "Passions do not exist" (J. VIII$_2$, 548). "Politics and literature do not exist for them" (VI, 567). "There is not a single moral power among them, not one name reiterated to me by fame" (VI, 567). And now, "the calling of the poet does not exist with us." The calling of the poet or the name of poet is a leitmotif in Chapters I and II. We read of Charsky: "In the magazines he was called a poet, in the servants' quarters, a scribbler"; "the unbearable *sobriquet*"; "However, he was a poet." There is, of course, a more narrowly sociological meaning to Charsky's remark, for he goes on to say "our poets do not enjoy the protection of patrons. Our poets are gentlemen in their own right." However, Charsky is naive, and it would be a simplification to restrict Pushkin's meaning to the professional. Pushkin is considering the "estate" of the poet which cannot be reduced to a class affair. He is taking up the issue of what one is "called" to be or do, hence one's name, *zvanie* (vs. *prozvishche*). In the final text Charsky is delighted that the Italian is an improvisor, and therefore can do without the title of poet. Pushkin removed from the drafts Charsky's ironic greeting "Signor Poeta" which gave too much away (J. VIII₂, 844). Names are not to be named, but the story aims to illustrate the calling of the poet. In the work of many poets there exists a distinction of roles which Blok once formulated as "the poet" and "the singer."[15] Charsky, the blithe and unconscious "singer," is in the midst of his seemingly irrelevant and irresponsible inspiration when the "poet" arrives on his doorstep, unbidden. It is the "calling of the poet" that Charsky tries so hard to escape.

Chapters I and II of "Egyptian Nights" contribute to the definition of this poet, mainly by means of allusions to Pushkin's own poems concerning him.[16] Echoes of "Poet"—the divided poet—have been universally noted in the characterization of Charsky. ("Before Apollo summons the poet to the holy sacrifice, he is perhaps the most insignificant of all the world's insignificant children" [III, 22; 1827].) The first improvisation also varies one other moment of that poem, significantly the moment which transforms the man into the poet, the decisive moment of the "word touching the ear." ("Poet": "But as soon as the divine word touches your keen ear..." [III, 22]; "Egyptian Nights": "Barely has someone else's thought touched your ear" [VI, 380].) "Such is the poet" repeats the conclusion of "Echo" (1831).

Any complete definition of the poet in "Egyptian Nights" must reach back to "The Poet and the Crowd" of 1828: "Like the wind his song is free, / But like the wind it is empty" (III, 87). By 1835 the poet-priest of 1828 has stepped from his pedestral and proudly accepted the crowd's formulation of his role—"a capricious wizard." He

108

adopts as a badge of honor his former rebuke to them: "You are the worm of the earth, not the son of the heavens." But "Egyptian Nights" remains the final commentary on these lines of 1828:

Brazenly turn to stone in your debauchery,
The voice of the lyre cannot bring you to life!
You are as repugnant as the tomb.

(III, 88)

The poet so defined is later displayed in action. Here the question of inspiration is naturally a crucial one. Many critics have sensed irony in the stylized romanticism of the passage which gives the final lift before the Cleopatra improvisation: "The improvisor already felt the approach of the god..." But with Pushkin's stylizations it is well to listen for the message carried by the style rather than always perceiving it as irony.[17] If we were to discount all of the stylistically colored passages of the story, there would be next to nothing left. This particular one suggests that the romantic poet is a role but a real and effective one, suited to the audience and to the moment. Those who say that Pushkin denies the improvisor any spiritual significance have misjudged the stylistic cues. Those who call him a *daimon* are closer to the source of his imaginative power in the story.[18]

But surely the Italian's rapture is still suspect? Pushkin's remarks of 1825 on the difference between inspiration and rapture have been applied to the distinction between Charsky and the improvisor in their creative states—Charsky possessing inspiration and the improvisor, rapture.

> *Inspiration?* That is the disposition of the soul towards the most lively reception of impressions, and consequently towards the rapid combination of ideas which facilitates their explanation. Inspiration is as necessary in poetry as in geometry. The critic confuses inspiration and rapture.
>
> ———
>
> No, definitely not: *rapture* excludes *repose*, which is the necessary condition of the *beautiful*. Rapture does not involve the power of mind which disposes the parts in their relation with the whole. Rapture is short-lived, intermitttent, thus unable to produce a true and great

109

perfection (without which there is no lyric poetry).[The argument concerns the ode.]
Rapture is the excited state of imagination alone. There can be inspiration without rapture, but rapture without inspiration does not exist.

(VII, 41)

It is nevertheless misleading to use this pronouncement to criticize the Italian; the opposition is not one between Charsky, the genuine artist, and the improvisor, the false artist.[19] Pushkin does not deny that ecstasy exists; he only objects to the idea of ecstasy apart from inspiration. The moment of being touched or rapt is a central one in "The Prophet," "Poet," and even for Mozart in "Mozart and Salieri": "genius... strikes a light about the head of the madman, / the idler... " (V, 359). This is the genius which, along with other absolute values, the Russian society in its positivism refuses to acknowledge. The Italian's rapture is not devoid of inspiration, which, Pushkin writes, has the power to bring together separate concepts in a way which tends to explain them. What else is the Cleopatra poem about the Egyptian nights which the Italian creates in response to the very scene before him? Here indeed is a power of mind working along with imagination which produces high lyric poetry—*liricheskaia poèziia.*

Thus, in the end, the Cleopatra improvisation of "Egyptian Nights" becomes the accessible manifestation of the imponderable that is inspiration. The audience of the salon society in the story was drawn to the improvisor's performance by the desire to be thrilled by poetic inspiration as a spectacle, by its "mechanics" as Charsky put it. But its real sources are left for the reader to discover. In the final analysis, "Egyptian Nights" as a whole is put at the service of a proof: an affirmation of the existence of passion and the moral powers, of history and literature, and also of the calling of the poet which makes the affirmation possible.

The World of Art

"Egyptian Nights" is more than an artist story, but to the extent that it incorporates one, how are we to take it? It is equally correct to read the story in two ways, one uplifting, the other sobering: first as the triumph of the independence of art and the fellowship of the poets, who are in the world but ultimately not of it; and secondly, as

110

the instructive tragedy of the poet as man who is threatened by his dependence on society, which though irrelevant to his art may even push him to the brink of disastrous adventure. Anyone who has reflected on the drama of Pushkin's last years will find these interpretations fully compatible. The story portrays the unenviable conditions under which Charsky and the improvisor must needs transcend the imperfect mortal state and become artists, enduring both the false adulation of society and its complete incomprehension of poetry. Clearly, though the artist story here has a social dimension, its point is not just that a poet is "really" a creature of his social class and not some ideal, not the "lyric hero of Russian romanticism."[20] Nevertheless, prevailing Soviet interpretations of the story stress how it "lowers" the romantic image of the poet as a glamorous creature privileged to live an existence as inspired as his art. Social characterizations of Charsky and the improvisor help to show that the artist is also a man like other men, and more generally that art and life are not one. Yet we must not overstate the social case lest we reduce the story to only one of its aspects. "Egyptian Nights" assumes a boundary fixed between life and art—and thus increases the tension between them. It even suggests that on rare occasions the boundary may be crossed (thus the Cleopatra anecdote passes into the Petersburg salon). Art itself remains one of the forms of the absolute, thus the Cleopatra story sets a standard by which life will be measured. As for the artist, to Pushkin he is a living paradox, now "low," now "high," bound to his social personality yet transcending it, and the story takes a perverse pleasure in the fact.

The aristocratic Charsky is all too quick to apply his social norms to the humble Italian, who is certainly no gentleman. Charsky hates to see him lower himself. Like Charsky, we "do not like to see the artist in the garb of a traveling showman," but there he is. The showman (*figliar*) could be a term of opprobrium, as with Pushkins's punning usage Figliarin for the hated Bulgarin whose antics degraded the profession of letters. But Charsky's phrase goes back to the so-called "Fragment" of 1830 which has rightly been associated with Pushkin's "Reply to Anonymous"[21] where the showman is treated sympathetically.

> Foolish is he who asks sympathy of society!
> The cold crowd regards the poet
> As a traveling showman: if he
> Gives deep expression to a heartfelt, heavy moan,
> And a verse born of suffering, penetratingly sad,

Strikes the heart with unheard-of force—
They clap their hands and praise him, or else
Shake their heads disapprovingly.

(III, 179)

In "Egyptian Nights" the improvisor is this *figliar*—that is, the poet as the crowd understands him. In "Reply to Anonymous" the *figliar* was Pushkin himself as understood by society.

The term was reiterated by Pushkin in his 1836 review "On Milton and Chateaubriand's Translation of *Paradise Lost*":

> We may be very mistaken, but Milton, on his way through Paris, would hardly have put himself on display like a traveling showman and amused society in the house of a woman of dubious reputation by reading verses written in a language unknown to any of those present, posing and taking on airs...

(VII, 495)

The full interest of this article for "Egyptian Nights" has perhaps not been grasped. Pushkin's angry commentary on Vigny's Milton stands in the background to the improvisor. The article for *The Contemporary*, indeed, protests against the artist as portrayed by the French romantics. Milton would not have behaved so, reading the elevated but not always elegant verse of *Paradise Lost* before mannered French society and in a language which they did not understand. That the improvisor does something analogous does not mean that he is the inferior kind of poet but rather that situated in the Russo-French high society, he has been miscast into a drama resembling those of the French romantics. The ardor of Pushkin's defense of Milton shows how personally he was touched by the spectacle of the miscast poet which threatened to become his own fate. Demonstratively, he used a traveling showman as one of his spokesmen in "Egyptian Nights," gave him the Cleopatra poem to declaim to an audience that did not understand his language in every sense of the phrase. His social circumstances can never lower him as an artist.

Art has not merely a social but also an absolute value in the story. It has again become poetry and not "literature" which indeed is impossible in the society setting. The society of "Egyptian Nights" reluctantly yields a meager choice of literary themes for the poet and fails to form an audience, the first prerequisites of literature as such. As the convention of the story has it, the improvisor's performance—Pushkin's Russian verse to the reader—represents only unintelligible Italian to the assembly in the hall. This shows us where the true audience lies, with the ideal reader. There is a progression that is not without its inner drama in the way that the buried poems of 1828 reassert themselves, first in the words of the "poet-friend" repeated by Aleksey Ivanych in "Evening at the Dacha," but eventually in the very act of creation by a poet in the flesh. The poet and the poem come increasingly to the foreground, and Cleopatra becomes the artist's theme. Both theme and character are treated in a fully self-conscious, even abstract way. The poem about Cleopatra now deliberately announces itself as a poem. Pushkin has also reached the limits of critical self-consciousness about his hero. He now defines him differently and not purely in social terms, though recognizing his social limitations. The hero is now at two removes from his beginnings—no longer the youth from the elegy, or even completely the man of the world, he is the poet. Pushkin rewrote the story a third time for the most complex of the personae which accompanied his life.

This means not only Charsky but also his alter ego, the Italian. True enough, he frequents the society world, but he is defined much more pertinently in terms of the style images in the story which embody a veritable world of art. (We have already spoken of the definition of a poet by means of allusions to Pushkin's lyrics about the craft.) With the Italian opera overture echoing behind him, the Neapolitan artist takes the stage. The improvisor speaks "a poor French," the language of society. He is surrounded by an aura of Hoffmanniana at first indistinguishable from the tinge of the *roman frénétique* (the "romantic" element). Pushkin himself had entertained a society gathering with a Hoffmannesque tale, "The Solitary Little House on Vasilevsky Island." The artist active in "Egyptian Nights" is not the *conteur* of Janin's *roman frénétique*. He has quasi-magical powers that make even the narrator of *Barnave* look weak. At moments he has to play the role of demonic double. His ancestry is probably German. The "almost translated" prose which Aleksey Ivanych spoke was translated from the French,[22] while the improvisor's soliloquy on art following the first improvisation has been associated with Tieck.[23] We naturally look to Hoffmann for the theme of the virtuoso performer. Pushkin once likened the author of an unsuccessful historical novel to the sorcerer's apprentice of Goethe's poem who could not control the "demon of the past" which he had conjured up (VII, 102). In the *conteur*/conversationalist there was not enough of the master sorcerer. If the story of the Cleopatra anecdote has an intrinsic "demonic" vitality of its own, then Pushkin needed an artist fitted to evoke it and loose it upon the Petersburg scene.

This brings us to the relations of art and life in the story. The apparent power of art over life in "Egyptian Nights" was one of the properties which attracted the symbolists to it. They saw realized in it the decadent idea that life imitates art—the repetition of the Cleopatra drama suggested by the improvisation—art, of course, being the higher or generative reality. Bryusov read the story's logic backward from poem to prose setting (after all, the poem was written first). However, Pushkin is not a member of the symbolist school, and the "swift" plots which he preferred have a strong forward momentum. It would be as true to say that the improvisation draws its inspiration from the social scene. In "Egyptian Nights" life imitates art and art, life, in a way which cannot definitively be disentangled.

Bryusov also interpreted the correspondences in the story as symbolic identity. Yet there is a gap between the fantastical and the symbolic. The historical correspondences generate the coincidences that give the reader pause, like the urn mentioned in the poem and also present in the room. The stereoscopic effect gives depth to the image, but its two parts remain separate. Correspondence or repetition does not necessarily mean identity or imply the existence of some eternal Platonic ideal. Indeed, it is unclear what identity would constitute, since all versions of the Cleopatra poem are open-ended. To the extent that the story reads "spatially" its images possess a sort of symbolism, that is, their interrelation appears to be inherent and the images lock together. To the extent that it reads "linearly" its images grow out of one another and remain free. The problem in the literary sense is that of Pushkin's use of parody in "Egyptian Nights," a symmetry relation that allows both rapprochements and discriminations. The symmetry of the pattern does threaten to close upon the characters with the trap-like precision of a nemesis plot.

This discussion has assumed that the internal patterning of "Egyptian Nights" at least matches its referential modeling in interest (matches the imitation of reality, the picturing of the society world and the poet's position within it, and so on). Aesthetic consciousness has outstripped realism; so it must appear to most modern readers.

The story has a mirror effect: the poet is doubled, he doubles Cleopatra and Petersburg doubles her Egyptian nights. Art holds up the mirror, and in it everything appears larger than life and more vivid, though oddly distanced. The aesthetic plane is flat, abstract and impersonal like fate, but also blindingly intense. The aesthetic seems to exist on its own terms: the vase in the drawing-room which echoes Cleopatra's urn no longer yields the lots of three lovers, but rather a choice of poetic themes. Still, as the Cleopatra theme unfolds so, too, does personal and historical reminiscence. A fiction with more latent life than the flesh and blood whose fantasy she is, Cleopatra rises to take possession of the plot. The lineaments of the Cleopatra poem are present three times in the design of "Egyptian Nights": once, in anticipation, when the Italian, like Cleopatra, addresses the audience; a second time bodily, as the verses of the improvisation; and finally, we presume, in parody/repetition, as projection onto the modern scene. Cleopatra is past, present and future.

There seems no escape from the anecdote whose vitality is ultimately frightening. We might even say that the dominance of the aesthetic in the story is an index of its pessimism. None of the themes available to the improvisor offer much comfort: the theme chosen, Cleopatra, the theme of the Decadence; the themes rejected—the Cenci, or the corruption of the family; the Last Day of Pompeii— apocalypse itself and a metaphor for political revolution; Spring seen from a Prison—*un*freedom in its classic form; the Triumph of Tasso—or the belated recognition by an ungrateful homeland of the poet 'on the edge of the grave.[24] At the moment before his performance the Italian himself appears rather sinister with his emphatically black theatrical attire and his funereal pallor. It is doubtful that the traveling showman has any elixir to offer, but the arsenic is likely to be genuine. Nothing in the story offers even the relenting reprieve of Cleopatra's last glance. Pushkin's ultimate triumph is to make the reader feel an acute pleasure in the prospect of destruction, feel how satisfying would be the catastrophe that the story prepares.

The Larger Picture

It would be misleading to suggest that the perspective of "Egyptian Nights" represented Pushkin's sole mental horizon in 1835. What remains is to give a brief outline of how the story fits into

115

the currents of his work that year, and more generally into the phenomenon of "late Pushkin." It is impossible to accomplish this with chronological precision since definite datings of single notebooks and a harmonization of datings for the many manuscripts which cluster around 1835 are not available.[25] Even within the "Egyptian Nights" cycle sequences are hypothetical. Renewed work on the cycle starts from a reprise of "A Tale from Roman Life" (begun in 1833). The impulse for this renewal may well reach back into 1834, to Pushkin's "Vesuvius opened its maw" and Bryullov's historical canvas. The draft of the "Roman Tale" includes both pen and pencil sections, indicating two work sessions, both of which may have fallen in 1833.[26] All that is certain is that in January, 1835, Pushkin wrote poems in classical stylization which fill a gap in "A Tale from Roman Life" (imitations of the anacreontic odes). Sometime towards the summer he also adapted a Horatian ode into "Which of the gods has restored to me" for the same story. The fragment "Evening at the Dacha" is said to date to "the first half of 1835 before 'Egyptian Nights.'"[27] As we remember, this implies the third "Cleopatra" as well, since its first draft is embedded in the sketch for that story.[28] It seems likely that "Evening at the Dacha" falls in the summer, "Egyptian Nights" finding a place in yet another Mikhaylovskoe autumn. The parameters which define "Egyptian Nights" enclose the period from the end of August/beginning of September, 1835 to the beginning of November of that year. This corresponds to the dates August 15 after "Scenes from the Days of Chivalry" and November 9 after the poem "When the Assyrian ruler." Apparently, the last part of "Egyptian Nights" to receive attention was the first improvisation "The poet comes, his eyes are open," for Pushkin's reworking of "Ezersky" dates to October/November. However, Pushkin did not always fill his notebooks consecutively and difficulties in dating make it possible to place "Why does sorrow oppress her," a later variant of the embedded third "Cleopatra," as late as 1836.[29] As Bryusov noted, Pushkin was still acquiring fresh Cleopatra materials then. It was in 1836 that he added to his library Jules de St. Félix's novel, *Cléopâtre: Reine d'Égypte.*[30]

Within these bounds we can examine the biographical and literary set which provides a context for the cycle and to some extent motivates it. We can detect a movement in the sequence from a revived society tale to the theme of the poet and observe that developments in 1835 are again capped by a piece of oriental stylization, "When the Assyrian ruler." (Compare "Cleopatra" in proximity to "The Upas-Tree" in 1828.) The "Egyptian Nights" cycle takes its place among a number of other retrospective ventures— looking back to the South, the journey and the end of *Eugene Onegin*. In January, 1835, pieces for "Table-Talk" deal with Kishinyov and the literary atmosphere of Pushkin's youth. The anacreontic odes for "A Tale from Roman Life" update the epicurean light-poetry ideal, and "Which of the gods has restored to me" works out reminiscences of 1825, of civic strife in Russia, not in Rome. The journey context which led into "A Tale from Roman Life" (the return from Arzrum) was active again: 1835 saw publication of *The Journey to Arzrum*. Two important traveler or wanderer poems belong to 1835: "Roderick" and also "The Wanderer" with its distant but still distinct evocation of the Pompeiian apocalypse of a city. ("*Nash gorod plameni i vetram obrechen*" III, 342.) Other poems explore the theme of "the death of the hero": "The Commander" with its suicide motif that Akhmatova found paralleled in "Evening at the Dacha,"[31] and "From A. Chénier," in which Hercules accepts the poisoned cloak from the envious centaur and lights his own funeral pyre. 1835 is also one of the anniversaries of *Poltava*, when Pushkin, writing his *History of Peter* returned to his heroic poem, chose an epigraph for it and wrote on the anniversary theme, "The Feast of Peter the Great." In the summer months of 1835, Pushkin lived again the dacha life which had inspired "Guests"; perhaps "Evening at the Dacha" was one result of this reminder. Another product of the summer months and transformation of the "poet at the dacha" is "Scenes from the Days of Chivalry" (dated August 15) with its hero, the unwilling troubadour who, imprisoned in the callous aristocratic castle, provides the entertainment prelude intended for his own execution. This work, too, is retrospective, leading back through the *Little Tragedies*, and its prose text incorporates "A Legend" of 1828 as one song interlude. The poet offends the bored Clotilda with his "low" passion. Plans for continuation suggest that the imprisoned, rebellious poet might have blown up the castle from the inside. We assume that "Egyptian Nights" followed on "Scenes from the Days of Chivalry" in close association with such openly retrospective poems as "Again have I visited" (September 26) and the fragment "I thought the heart had forgotten." "Egyptian Nights" also revived in conjunction with a tentative revival of *Eugene Onegin*. Perhaps the novel was, in fact, open-ended, and Pushkin might have gone on from there ("In my autumn leisure," III, 355/475-76, September 16). But though Pushkin rejected the idea, which seemed to cast him as a

117

society entertainer (see the above discussion of the *figliar*), "Egyptian Nights" does take up from the end of *Onegin*, from its final society picture (Nina Voronskaya—the Cleopatra of the Neva). If "Egyptian Nights" ties back to the old novel in Pushkin, it also has certain affinities with the embryonic new novel known as "A Russian Pelham" (1834 or later), the successor to *Eugene Onegin* and the alternative to *The Captain's Daughter*, the historical novel. The wide-ranging plan for this ambitious work included the hero's introduction as a youth into high society, a liaison with a society woman and the counterbalancing but also dangerous attractions of the Bohemian milieu ("bad society," "*la mauvaise société*"). Broadly speaking, "A Russian Pelham" is satirical and takes its place, along with "Egyptian Nights," next to satires executed in classical or biblical stylization—"On the Recovery of Lucullus,"[32] and finally, "When the Assyrian ruler."

The literary fact of 1835 which bulks largest in Pushkin's production is, of course, the set of notebooks for his *History of Peter*. It might appear that literature proper was outweighed that year by history. It would be more accurate to say that the historical in Pushkin is a category larger than fiction and non-fiction and encompasses both. By the end of 1834 Pushkin had set aside *The Captain's Daughter*, the Scott historical novel, but published its corollary, *The History of Pugachyov*. The year 1835 saw him pursuing the complementary line, *The History of Peter*, coordinated with a variety of shallow-retrospect conceptions which group around the general theme of a "history of my times."[33] There is the low road of the Scott historical novel, history made from below, history domesticated where the family chronicle and the common man prevail. Then there is the high road of history made from above, of great men and consciousness. Both historical roads involve stylization in Pushkin's fiction. *The Captain's Daughter* is told in a deliberately old-fashioned eighteenth-century voice. It realizes Pushkin's well-known threat in *Eugene Onegin* to write the "*starinnyi roman.*" "Scenes from the Days of Chivalry" only displaces the situation of *The Captain's Daughter* from which "Egyptian Nights" further branches off—that of the aristocratic renegade poet. In the broadest perspective on Pushkin, one could say that a "style of antiquity" incorporated into "Egyptian Nights" from "A Tale from Roman Life" is contrasted to a "style of olden times." The two streams in 1835 are represented by classical/biblical stylizations, on the one hand, and documentation for Petrine history on the other.

118

The society tale is adapted to the westernized society which Russia inherited from Peter. This for Pushkin is the story of his times. "The drawing-room novel is the novel of our age," as Vyazemsky said of *Adolphe*.[34] "Egyptian Nights" is a Petersburg tale. Chronologically and logically it fits inside *The History of Peter* as "Guests"did within *Poltava*.

In 1834 Pushkin had put aside *The Captain's Daughter*. In it, a recast sentimental novel just manages to defeat a romantic robber plot. The hero eludes the phantom scaffold floating down the Volga. (The sentimental comes *after* the romantic, as softened feeling should in the Cleopatra elegy.) In *The Captain's Daughter* history was to be made into an ideal realm—the past of the pardoned renegade to which the maturing generation of the grandsons could look back over the heads of their ruined fathers. *The Captain's Daughter* creates a positive genealogy and subdues that special "demon of the past" which the history of the eighteenth century represented to Pushkin, who found much that was congenial in Radishchev's bitter "*Os'mnadtsatoe stoletie*." In 1835 he had not found the complete solution, which was only valid, besides, in the sphere of the Scott historical novel. "Egyptian Nights" takes place, as we know, in a society that has forgotten its ancestors, for whom its own history does not exist. Such a society is naturally defenseless against what we might call the "demon of antiquity." This demon it is that Pushkin set out to harness in his "Egyptian Nights" which unfold in Peter's northern capital.

The past which informs "Egyptian Nights" is like the time perspective in the other Petersburg tales, *The Bronze Horseman* and "The Queen of Spades." It is an evil enchantment. An amnesia reigns from which it is impossible to recover anything satisfactory (Evgeny's forgetful ramblings, the game *oubli ou regret* and the Countess' blank stare). At crucial moments the flow of time is even reversed. Witness: "The Neva flowed backward" (IV, 386); or Herman's appearance in the Countess' eighteenth-century boudoir like one of the former lovers of the "Muscovite Venus." Time threatens to move back into a frozen past, refusing to go forward into the future. The themes in "Egyptian Nights," like the cards in "The Queen of Spades," are not really prophetic. We face a situation like the game of patience recounted in "The Solitary Little House on Vasilevsky Island"— upon which the demonic brother Bartholomew, a distant prototype of the improvisor, comments:

The old woman set to her favorite evening pastime—fortune-telling with cards. But however she tried to lay them out—as if to spite her nothing came of it. Bartholomew came up to her...Seeing the annoyance of the old woman he remarked to her that by her method of laying them out you could not tell the future, and the cards, as they were now disposed, showed the past. "Oh, my Lord! I see you are a master; explain it to me, what do they show then?" the old woman asked with a dubious look. "Well, this," he answered, and drawing up a chair talked softly for a long time. What did he say? God only knows...

(IX, 514)

Lednicki once remarked that Pushkin was "Old Testament" by temperament. "Egyptian Nights" seems by affinity to range itself with his works of retribution and not redemption, finally belying the softening of Cleopatra's elegy. And for all the pressing toward the future and toward the younger generation amply attested to in late Pushkin, "Egyptian Nights" exists as one reminder of the pessimistic alternative, in which the artist was not always able to subdue the "demons of the past," or to shape his vision to progressive ends.

CONCLUSION

This completes the creative history of Pushkin's "Egyptian Nights" that began in 1824 with a remark on Aurelius Victor and the poem "Cleopatra." The history unfolded in three stages: formation in 1824, when the psychological problem was central, development in 1828-30 along the lines of biography or social commentary; condensation in 1833 and 1835 and infusion with historical, philosophical and aesthetic problems. Pushkin wrote the Cleopatra story for three successive heroes: first, the youth, then, the man of the world, and finally, the poet. His Cleopatra accompanied them but changed in less essential ways, even as society heroine. In 1824 the divided character of Cleopatra was set off by the youth, her third lover; in 1828, by the provincial girl of the plan for "Guests." In 1833 and 1835, the period whose spirit Cleopatra embodied was explicitly defined as the Decadence, a historical concept which implies a boundary with a new age; and, finally, in "Egyptian Nights" itself, Cleopatra was paired with the poets. At none of these stages was the artistic aim to present only the incarnation of lust, cruelty and satiety.

From the psychological tension of the original historical elegy, its paradox of compassion, sprang the lifeline of the entire cycle, characterized by the pathos of a desire for renewal balanced against the expectation of a fatal reckoning. The animation which Cleopatra had imparted to her feast, and which Volskaya had restored to jaded high society, found its ultimate expression in the dynamic action of the improvisation, where it is the poet as mover who attempts to leaven the inert social mass. The largely decorative historical side of the 1824 poem "Cleopatra" was discarded in 1828 for a contemporary tale with an emphasis on the biographical past of its characters. Then it re-emerged in 1833 and 1835 as continuous historical stylization, only to be absorbed into the parodistic plan of "Evening at the Dacha," in the possibility of historical repetition. In "Egyptian Nights," the past of antiquity meets the present of Petersburg society through the mediation of the Italian improvisor, but historical repetition is possible there only because a true consciousness of history is absent, because the time of the story is the *bezvremen'e*, the "dead time" of the Russian/Egyptian nights.

Certain outside influences, really literary stimuli, helped to move the cycle forward. Aurelius Victor's ancedote and Parny's

Persephone from the "Déguisements de Vénus" contributed to its formation; then came Baratynsky's *Ball*, Janin's *Barnave*, Petronius' *Satyricon* and Tacitus' *Annals*, the Cleopatra of Shakespeare and of Plutarch, the wit of Madame de Staël, and the fantasy of E.T.A. Hoffmann. French, German, Italian and classical style-images overlap in "Egyptian Nights." The general conversation which the poets come to conduct there in place of the public shared its critical terms with Chaadaev's pessimistic *Philosophical Letters*. The night which witnessed their exchange entered the annals of other such "nights" and "evenings": Batyushkov's "An Evening with Kantemir," Maistre's *Saint Petersburg Evenings*, Odoevsky's *Russian Nights*.

The development of the cycle can also be seen in terms of genre: the mixed "historical elegy" of 1824 containing the possibilities of the erotic ballad, of drama and of satire found new incarnations first in the analytic society tale, then in a historically stylized Satyricon, really a form of philosophical prose, and, finally, in the artist story. All three narratives strongly involved lyrical and dramatic modes of presentation: in "Guests," the balcony scene and figurative social stage; in "A Tale from Roman Life," the public declamation of the odes which formed part of the Satyricon; in "Egyptian Nights," the device of the improvisations. In the end the approach of parody offered the closest equivalent to the ambiguity of the original psychological situation, but expressed as plot.

This is the new analytic prose of a poet, in which thought has been reabsorbed into style and form and in which the most disturbing personal complexes have been made objective. Akhmatova felt that fragments like "A Tale from Roman Life" or "Evening at the Dacha" rivalled the *Little Tragedies* in their laconic, concentrated power.[1] At Pushkin's death, his friends were amazed to discover that this man of letters had continued to develop as a poet. Annenkov later commented: "In the unpublished verse you can see how the phenomena of life begin to present themselves to his mind under an aspect which somehow lies in proximity to a historical or religious idea."[2] Yet "Cleopatra" had always been a philosophical poem about the value of life, echoing the cry, "did it not all come down to one or two nights?" The final story of 1835 is simply one last statement about those few nights, made with a fuller consciousness of the things that make them count.

It is now possible to see how this succession of literary realizations of the Cleopatra theme emerged from the dynamic of Pushkin's unfolding work. In 1824 the original conception was born of the disintegration of the "southern poems," side by side with the "Imitations of the Koran." It also shared important motifs and something of the moral atmosphere of a central ballad complex about "the bridegroom." In the middle stage of the development, "Guests," the Cleopatra material was drawn into the evolution of *Onegin*. Stanzas from Onegin's "Journey" and from his "Album" led to the point of departure for "Guests," whose arrangement of characters anticipated, in turn, the final grouping of Chapter VIII in *Onegin*, where the "brilliant Nina Voronskaya, that Cleopatra of the Neva" was seated beside Tatyana in the society salon. "Guests" also clearly recapitulated Chapter I of the novel in verse, set in the world of Petersburg society. The pair of heroes whose presence would be the mark of all the further Cleopatra stories appeared for the first time in "Guests," out of the sphere of *Onegin*, where in Chapter I the hero was doubled by his friend, the narrator, and where the pair Onegin and Lensky represented the clash of prose and poetry. In addition, the Cleopatra intrigue of "Guests" was intertwined in its genesis with the writing of Maria's love story in *Poltava*, another use of the bridegroom ballad. "Guests" was thus situated in the manuscripts between the historical and the contemporary, between *Poltava* and *Onegin*. The next stage in the development of the Cleopatra material was influenced by reflections arising out of the *The Journey to Arzrum*. It was at this point in the history of the cycle that an artistic image connected with Egypt first appeared, the "Egyptian tombs." The return from Arzrum left its mark on "Guests" (1830), "A Tale from Roman Life," and the so-called "Fragment" which was later revised for the characterization of Charsky. The end of *Onegin* and the return from Arzrum were the creative events that shaped the middle of the Cleopatra cycle, acting to highlight the arrival of a moment of fate, which might bring either retribution or renewal.

Like "Scenes from the Days of Chivalry" or indeed *The Captain's Daughter*, the Cleopatra fragments of 1835 are works of the renegade poet who threatens the aristocratic establishment from the inside. However, the end of the cycle was governed less by any new connections with other works of Pushkin than by what might be termed the aesthetic event of indirection. Pushkin developed and varied the figure of the "conversationalist" who had been mentioned in an 1828 draft of "Guests"—first in Petronius, then in Aleksey Ivanych and finally in the Italian improvisor. In the place of conversations are put various kinds of performances, and, meanwhile, the poem "Cleopatra" which was buried or perhaps dissolved in "Guests" is restored to independent life. The overall sequence was poetry into prose, then prose again into poetry. Under its final aspect, the poetry is meant to be sensed precisely as such, as something poetic with a power to move and magically to animate. The poetic improvisations return in their function to the very first line of the original Cleopatra poem, in which the queen "with voice and glance animated her luxurious feast."

Tynyanov once wrote, "The concept of breadth of genre range turns out to be less fundamental with respect to Pushkin than is the rapid and even catastrophic evolution of his work."[3] He wished to direct attention away from the undoubted scope and universality of Pushkin to the impetuous unfolding of the writer's creation. However, in the case of the history of the Cleopatra material, as with any cycle, the development was also in a sense circular. Akhmatova remarked upon the fact that the plots and imaginative patterns of Pushkin's works in the 1830's often were derived from strata of experience laid down ten years earlier or more. The patterns "settled" or clarified but were not replaced by new ones.[4] The later stages of the Cleopatra cycle are likewise notable for the way in which aspects of earlier Pushkin persist and are reinterpreted, a process for which parody is an inadequate term unless parody is understood partly as a creative rather than a destructive relationship. "A Tale from Roman Life" witnessed a revival of Pushkin's interest in the Roman historians, in anacreontic verse and in the occasion of the poetic feast. "Evening at the Dacha" presented its Cleopatra poem as a fragment from an unfinished romantic narrative poem. The opening lines of the poem echoed "Reminiscence," and a harem scene re-emerged from the buried layer of the "southern poems." In "Egyptian Nights," the Cleopatra improvisation was based on a theme suggested by the Petersburg poet, whose dandified existence calls to mind Onegin's; it also represented an auto-reminiscence of the author's own poetry.

The retrospective elements in late Pushkin are best perceived as romantic stylization—as part of the author's own artistic repertoire and not as purely polemical in application. In "Evening at the Dacha" the Cleopatra poem still represented something genuine, something literally true, something quite opposed to the fashionable rantings of the "new novels." The "ornamental" quality of the 1835 "Cleopatra" served to persuade its doubting audience of the reality of the scenes and events depicted in the poem. In its turn, the first improvisation in "Egyptian Nights" defended a form of "romantic realism," based only on a radical freedom from all convention. Of course, the Cleopatra anecdote itself possessed a life-or-death seriousness. Thus, as Bocharov has written in another context, in the development of Pushkin's work "poetic tradition" (*poèticheskoe predanie*) does not become outworn; rather it acquires the force of literal truth.[5] When Pushkin turned again to the Cleopatra anecdote in 1835, he touched one of the "nerve-centers of long-accumulated poetic energy."[6]

The self-contained literary quality of "Egyptian Nights," along with its problems of modernity and decadence, of periods of transition, give the work a contemporary relevance. The split time perspective and, above all, the multi-layered narrative structure of the story (or really story within a story) lend it a strong appeal for the twentieth-century reader and writer. The story fuses personal reminiscence, historical reminiscence, and literary reminiscence into a single whole; the poem conceived in 1824 retains a personal meaning for the story's poet, but one overlaid by the perspective of historical repetition and the poetic spell cast by the ancient anecdote. But the almost crystalline symmetry of the form in which the story is cast, and the relentless logic of the artistic syllogism upon which it is built, these qualities belong to Pushkin alone. "Egyptian Nights" shows the writer enmeshed in a situation of potentially tragic compromise, the writer who is beleaguered by the "social command" to which he responds whether he wills or no. It displays a writer who is isolated and faced with a silent audience, one who communicates within the privileged but restricted community of the poets. The fragment, belying its fragmentary nature, contains the complete expression of a continuing and perhaps haunted predicament.

Afterlife

The sequels of Hofman and Bryusov aside, Pushkin's Cleopatra and the Egypt of his "Egyptian Nights" possess a notable afterlife in Russian literature. The story was even choreographed as a ballet by Fokine (*A Night in Egypt*, 1908), performed as a pantomine in Nemirovich-Danchenko's studio (1928) and later included in a pastiche of Cleopatra stories by the Chamber Theater (1936). Prokofiev, too, composed a musical suite entitled *Egyptian Nights*.[7] The fashion for "Egyptian Nights" launched by the symbolist adaptations would seem to have been reinforced later by the Egyptomania inspired by the discovery of the tomb of Tutankhamen in 1922. But there was more than fashion to the longevity of the Cleopatra legend and of the theme of Egyptian nights in Russia, for they served as an expression of the difficult situation of the Russian poet and also as an image of the Russian historical condition.

Egypt had gained a new mystical notoriety after Vladimir Solovyov's vision of Sophia, the Wisdom of God, in the desert near Cairo. It was this Egypt of the symbolist generation which found its final expression in Merezhkovsky's historical romances *The Mystery of the Three: Egypt and Babylon* (Prague, 1925) and *The Birth of the Gods: Tutankhamen on Crete* (Prague, 1926). Rozanov devloped another image of Egypt, an idiosyncratic, positive one, in his *From Oriental Motifs* (Petrograd, 1916-18). But the Alexandrian Egypt of the Decadence and the Egypt of the inert necropolis remained a persistent mythological construct for modern Russian literature. Alexandria was the setting for Bryusov's erotic ballads about Cleopatra (in *Tertia Vigilia* and *Stephanos*) and for Kuzmin's "Alexandrian Songs" (*Nets*, 1906). The Egypt as necropolis appears appropriately in Bely's *Petersburg*, in the epilogue where Nikolay Ableukhov forgets his disastrous rebellion by absorbing himself in reading the *Book of the Dead* at the foot of the Sphinx. The Sphinx recalls the Petersburg sphinxes of the Neva embankment, which Pudovkin was to capture in a significant shot for his film *The End of Petersburg*. Mandelstam, in his own story of the end of an epoch in Petersburg, "The Egyptian Stamp," wrote that the Theban sphinxes were one of the favorite meeting places of the Petersburg population. In the essay "The Nineteenth Century," he explained: "In the veins of our century flows the heavy blood of extremely distant monumental cultures, perhaps Egyptian and Assyrian..."[8] Bank buildings have "Egyptian porticoes,"[9] and even the insignificant mosquito, one of the hero's doubles in "The Egyptian Stamp," whines:

> —Look what has happened to me: I am the last Egyptian—a sobber sober tutor, simple soldier—I am a little bow-legged prince—a beggarly, blood-sucking Rameses—in the north I have become nothing—so little is left of me—I beg your pardon!
> —I am the prince of ill fortune—a collegiate assessor of the city of Thebes...[10]

Although these Egyptian motifs are not textually derived from Pushkin's "Egyptian Nights," they resonate with the orientation set by the story. As Khlebnikov once commented of his own very different Egyptian tale, "Ka," "I struck a harmonious note to

'Egyptian Nights,' the attraction of the snowstorm of the North to the Nile and its tropical heat."[11]

Still, it was Pushkin's "Cleopatra" as presented in "Egyptian Nights" which made an indelible impression upon the creative imagination of Russian poets. Blok and Akhmatova each wrote a Cleopatra poem which announces its filiation with Pushkin. In Blok's "Cleopatra" of 1907 the poet is ranged *with* the crowd which gapes at the waxen figure of Cleopatra, lying before them in a state of suspended animation. Eternally consumed by her satiety, she is still able to hurl a cruel taunt at the poet. While the crowd whispers obscene remarks, the poet alone is moved at the sight of the Egyptian queen. But the poet has been fatally debased, he is "shameful and venal." Like the improvisor he was a slave, but now feels himself "a poet and king." Cleopatra, once a queen, has become "wax, corruption and dust." This debased queen will have her revenge on the debased poet: she will make a mockery of his poetic dreams. "Russia, like Rome, is drunk with her"; but the repetition turns into the bitterest parody. Such is Blok's interpretation of Cleopatra and her poet.

Cleopatra

The sad panopticon's been open
One, two, three years.
We hurry, a drunken, brazen mob,
The queen waits in her coffin.

She rests in a glass coffin,
Neither dead nor alive,
And people tirelessly whisper
Shameless words about her.

She lies lazily stretched out—
Only to forget and never wake—
The serpent, easy and unhurried,
Bites her waxen breast...

I myself, shameful and venal,
With blue circles under my eyes,
Have come to glimpse the solemn profile,
The wax laid out on show...

127

Everyone inspects you,
But if your coffin were not empty,
I should have heard more than once
The proud sigh of lips mouldered away:

"Waft me with incense. Strew flowers.
In untold ages past
I was queen in Egypt.
Now I am wax. I am corruption. I am dust."

"O queen! I am in your power!
In Egypt I was but a slave,
But now by fate's decree
I am a poet and a king!

Can you see now from your coffin
That Russia, like Rome, is drunk with you?
That I and Caesar will both be
Equal through the ages before destiny?"

I speak no more. I look. She does not hear.
But her breast barely trembles
And breathes behind the filmy cloth...
I hear the quiet words:

"Then, I hurled the thunder.
Now, I shall wrench out, bitter-hot,
A drunken poet's tears,
A drunken prostitute's laughter."[12]

In his article of 1910, "On the Present State of Russian Symbolism," Blok developed the significance of Cleopatra's fate, expanded on his understanding of the frozen moment with which he began the poem of 1907, the moment when Cleopatra has taken the asp to her breast. Cleopatra, like the symbolist generation, says Blok, has chosen submissive death rather than heroic struggle:

All of us were taken up, as it seemed, onto a high mountain, from whence the kingdoms of the world lay before us bathed in the undreamt-of radiance of a purple sunset; we surrendered to the sunset, beautiful as queens, but not handsome as kings, and fled from the heroic deed. That was why it was so easy for the uninitiated to rush after us, that is why symbolism is discredited. We dissolved in the world the "pearl of love." But Cleopatra was the Queen of Kings only until the

128

hour when passion made her lay the serpent to her breast. Either death in submission or a feat of courage.[13]

Akhmatova, in her Cleopatra poem of 1940, starts from the same point of departure, the asp at the breast, but she understands Cleopatra's death to be a tragic and courageous act. Her Cleopatra, who is a queen to the end, becomes a powerful image which might well represent Russia or the poet herself, bereaved, persecuted, betrayed, but ultimately undaunted before the tyrant Augustus, refusing to become a slave-girl to be displayed in his triumphal procession. Her anonymous last lover has unwittingly confirmed her resolve to die. Akhmatova's Cleopatra is modeled after Shakespeare's, but the implied presence in her poem of Russia's recent past and the understood parallel with the fate of the poet direct our attention to the epigraph from Pushkin, "sweet shadow fell over the palaces of Alexandria." These are lines taken from the 1835 Cleopatra poem, and printed to this day after the 1828 text in "Egyptian Nights" as Pushkin's possible continuation of the fragment "Cleopatra" (VI, 389). Akhmatova's poem thus presents yet another significant interpretation of the outcome of the Cleopatra story, presented not as a symbolist's eternal drama, but as one turn of the wheel in the cyclical movement which governs the historical fate of Russia and her poets.

Cleopatra

I am air and fire...
Shakespeare

Sweet shadow fell
Over the palaces of Alexandria.
Pushkin

She has already kissed Antony's dead lips,
Already shed tears on her knees before Augustus...
And the servants have betrayed her. The victory trumpets blare
Beneath the Roman eagle, and the evening mist descends.

Now enters the last one enthralled by her beauty,
Tall and imposing, and he whispers in confusion:
"He sends you—like a slave-girl—before him in the triumph..."
But her swan-neck curves, just as calm.

Tomorrow they slaughter the children. O, how little remains
For her to do on this earth—to jest with a peasant
And lay the black snake, like a last mercy,
On her swarthy breast with indifferent hand.[14]

NOTES

Quotations from Pushkin are identified (1) from A. S. Pushkin, *Polnoe sobranie sochinenii*, 3rd ed. (Moscow, 1962-66); (2) in the case of drafts and variants not found there, from the Jubilee edition, A. S. Pushkin, *Polnoe sobranie sochinenii* (M.-L., 1937-49); (3) in the case of citation from *Eugene Onegin*, by chapter and stanza. With the exception of Clarence Brown's *Mandelstam*, all translations are my own. They do not claim independent literary merit, especially where verse is concerned. Readers will find the Russian text to the poems in the Appendix. English translations of "Egyptian Nights" include: *The Poems, Prose and Plays of Alexander Pushkin*. Avrahm Yarmolinsky, ed. N.Y.: Random House Modern Library, 1936; *The Complete Prose Tales of Alexandr Sergeyevitch Pushkin*, Gillon R. Aitken, tr. N.Y.: Norton, 1966; *Alexander Pushkin: Complete Prose Fiction*. Paul Debreczeny, tr. Stanford: Stanford Univ. Press, 1983; D. M. Thomas, *Ararat*. N. Y.: Viking, 1983, pp. 51-68.

Notes: Introduction

[1]V. Briusov, "Egipetskie nochi," in *Sobranie sochinenii* (M., 1974), III, 438-54 (originally published 1916). Modest L. Hofman, *Egipetskie nochi* (Paris, 1935).

[2]P. V. Annenkov, *A. S. Pushkin: Materialy dlia ego biografii i otsenki proizvendenii* (S. Pbg., 1873), p. 387.

[3]See N. I. Zheltov, M. I. Kolesnikov and N. K. Piksanov, eds., *Tvorcheskaia istoriia proizvedenii russkikh i sovetskikh pisatelei: Bibliograficheskii ukazatel'* (M.: Kniga, 1968).

[4]S. Bondi, "O chtenii rukopisei Pushkina," in *Chernoviki Pushkina: Stat'i 1930-1970 gg.* (M., 1971), pp. 144-45, 165. The article was written in 1932.

[5]D. S. Likhachev, "Zadachi tekstologii," *Russkaia literatura* (1961, No. 4), pp. 175-76.

[6]See E. D. Lebedeva, *Tekstologiia russkoi literatury XVIII-XX vv.: Ukazatel' sovetskikh rabot na russkom iazyke 1917-1975* (M.: Nauka, 1978).

[7]V. Khodasevich, *Poèticheskoe khoziaistvo Pushkina* (L.: Mysl', 1924) and Anna Akhmatova, *O Pushkine: Stat'i i zametki*, ed. È. G. Gershtein (L.: Sov. Pis., 1977).

[8]S. Bondi, "K istorii sozdaniia 'Egipetskikh nochei,'" in *Novye stranitsy Pushkina* (M., 1931), pp. 148-205.

[9]B. V. Tomashevskii, "Tekst stikhotvoreniia Pushkina 'Kleopatra,'" *Uchenye zapiski LGU*, No. 200, Seriia filologicheskikh nauk, vyp. 25 (1955), pp. 216-29.

[10]M. Gorlin, "'Noce egipskie' (Kompozycja i Geneza)," in *Puszkin*, ed. W. Lednicki (Krakow, 1939), I, 128-45. E. Chirpak-Rozdina, "'Egipetskie nochi' A. S. Pushkina," *Studia Slavica*, T. 19, fascicle 4 (Budapest, 1973), 373-90.

[11]According to Chirpak-Rozdina this resulted from the ostensible interference between the representation of socially conditioned psychology and the simultaneous depiction of eternal psychological verities in "Egyptian Nights" (p. 384). The dilemma is perhaps more artificial than real.

[12]B. V. Tomashevskii, *Pisatel' i kniga*, 2nd ed. (M.: Iskusstvo, 1959), p. 153.

[13]Likhachev, p. 177.

[14]V. I. Kuleshov, ed., *Zamysel, trud, voploshchenie* (M.: MGU, 1977), p. 8.

[15]Tomashevskii, *Pisatel' i kniga*, p. 88.

[16]G. Vinokur, *Kritika poèticheskogo teksta* (M.: Gos. akad. khud. nauk, 1927), p. 43.

[17]See, for example, B. Gasparov, I. Paperno, "K opisaniiu motivnoi struktury liriki Pushkina," and A. K. Zholkovskii, "Materialy k opisaniiu poèticheskogo mira Pushkina," in *Russian Romanticism: Studies in the Poetic Code*, ed. Nils Ake Nilsson (Stockholm: Almqvist and Wiksell, 1979), pp. 9-45, 45-94. Also Savely Senderovich, "K rekonstruktsii

poėticheskoi mifologii Pushkina (Fenomenologicheskii ėtiud)," *Wiener slavistischer Almanach*, vol. 7 (1981), pp. 5-36.

[18]Tomashevskii, *Pisatel' i kniga*, pp. 107-08. B. V. Tomashevskii, "Izdaniia stikhotvornykh tekstov," *Literaturnoe nasledstvo*, XVI-XVIII, pp. 1059-60.

[19]Tomashevskii, "Izdaniia," p. 1108.

[20]B. Meilakh, *Khudozhestvennoe myshlenie Pushkina kak tvorcheskii protsess* (M.: Nauka, 1962), p.6.

Notes: Chapter I

[1]B. V. Tomashevskii, *Pushkin* (M.-L., 1961), II, 55.

[2]*Ibid.*, II, 57.

[3]Sextus Aurelius Victor, *De Viris Illustribus Romae*, Cap. LXXXVI, 2.

[4]Tomashevskii, *Pushkin*, II, 57.

[5]There has never been a serial publication of the Pushkin manuscripts in their notebook form. With one exception, a published notebook for 1833-34, only those with access to the manuscripts or photocopies and who also possess a professional textological and paleographic training are in a position to reconstruct the flow of texts and fragments which can fall within a single notebook or be scattered among several roughly contemporary ones. Others must settle for a compromise. I have used the description of the 1824 notebook which Bondi presented in 1931 in his textological article on "Egyptian Nights," filling in on a chronological basis from datings in M. A. Tsiavlovskii, *Letopis' zhizni i tvorchestva A. S. Pushkina*, (M.-L., 1951), I, and for later years in N. O. Lerner, *Trudy i dni Pushkina*, 2nd ed. (S. Pbg., 1910), checking the datings against those accepted in the two standard editions of Pushkin (the Jubilee and the latest ten-volume). Datings, of course, are not of the same value as information about actual positions in the manuscripts. Occasionally I have been fortunate in finding a relevant notebook plotted out in an article that seeks to place other works.

[6]See L. S. Fleishman, "Iz istorii ėlegii v pushkinskuiu ėpokhu," *Pushkinskii sbornik*, Uchenye zapiski, Latviiskii gos. univ. imeni Petra Stuchki, No. 106 (Riga, 1968), pp. 24-54. Also L. G. Frizman, *Zhizn' liricheskogo zhanra: Russkaia ėlegiia ot Sumarokova do Nekrasova* (M.: Nauka, 1973).

[7]Tomashevskii, *Pushkin*, I, 389, 492.

[8]An observation confirmed recently by N. N. Petrunina, in "'Egipetskie nochi'i russkaia povest' 1830-kh godov," *Pushkin: Issledovaniia i materialy*, VIII (L.: Nauka, 1978), 23.

[9]According to the notes in the Jubilee edition (following S. Bondi, "K istorii sozdaniia 'Egipetskikh nochei,'" in *Novye stranitsy Pushkina* [M., 1931], pp. 202-03), the 1824 version of "Cleopatra" was written as follows: lines 1-58 between the 2nd and 9th of October, lines 59-63 between the 10th and the 15th, lines 64-70 around the 1st of November (J. II, 1170). The Jubilee states that *Gypsies* was begun in January, 1824; the first 145 lines were written before Pushkin's departure for Mikhailovskoe on July 30; the rest, between the 2nd and 10th of October. By October 8, *Gypsies* had been finished except for the epilogue which was written and revised by the time the fair copy was made on October 10 (J. IV, 472).

[10]Ia. Bagdasariants was the first to notice this in "K istorii teksta 'Egipetskikh nochei,'" *Pushkin: Stat'i i materialy*, (Odessa: Odesskii dom uchenykh, 1926), II, 88-91.

[11]T. G. Tsiavlovskaia mentions the connection between "Persephone" and "Cleopatra" without enlarging on its significance, in "Khrani menia, moi talisman," *Prometei*, No. 10 (M., 1974), pp. 35-38.

[12]Bondi, p. 157.

[13]Anna Akhmatova, *O Pushkine*, ed. Ė. G. Gershtein, (L.: Sov. Pis., 1977), pp. 211, 212.

[14]As quoted in Russian by M. N. Kovalenskii, *Puteshestvie Ekateriny II v Krym*, 2nd ed. (M., 1920), p. 67.

[15]L. Grossmann, *Pushkin v teatral'nykh kreslakh* (M., 1928), p. 249.

[16]M. Zagorskii, *Pushkin i teatr* (M.-L., 1940), pp. 66-69. On theatrical elements in

"Cleopatra," see also S. V. Shervinskii, "Iz 'Egipetskikh nochei,'" in his *Ritm i smysl* (M., 1961), pp. 142, 147, 152.

[17] *Domik v Kolomne*, unpublished stanzas (IV, 527).

[18] I reproduce the text of the 1828 "Cleopatra" as published in the ten-volume edition. Tomashevskii in his 1955 article argued that the editions current until then had improperly transposed sections of the poem, and his emendation was accepted. B. V. Tomashevskii, "Tekst stikhotvoreniia Pushkina 'Kleopatra,'" *Uchenye zapiski LGU*, No. 200, Seriia filologicheskikh nauk, vyp. 25 (1955), pp. 216-29. Tomashevskii discusses all of the versions of the poem together in his chapter "Cleopatra," *Pushkin*, II, 55-65. Pages 55-58 deal with the shape of the poem before 1835.

[19] V. Briusov, "Egipetskie nochi," *Moi Pushkin* (M.-L, 1929), p. 118.

[20] "Table-Talk," VIII, 90-91.

[21] Khodasevich wittily confirms the connection between the three lovers of *Ruslan and Liudmila* and "Cleopatra" in his *Poèticheskoe khoziaistvo Pushkina* (L., 1924), p. 12.

[22] M. O. Gershenzon, *Mudrost' Pushkina* (M., 1919), pp. 69-81.

[23] Tomashevskii "Tekst," pp. 218, 225.

[24] Bruisov, pp. 115-16.

[25] Briusov, p. 113.

[26] Tomashevskii, *Pushkin*, II, pp. 58-59.

[27] *Ibid.*, p. 58.

[28] F. M. Dostoevskii, *Polnoe sobranie sochinenii v tridtsati tomakh*, XIX (L.: Nauka, 1979), 136-37 ("Otvet *Russkomu vestniku*," 1861). See V. Ia. Kirpotin, "Dostoevskii o 'Egipetskikh nochakh' Pushkina," *Voprosy literatury*, (1962, No. 11), pp. 112-22.

[29] P. V. Annenkov, *A. S. Pushkin: Materialy dlia ego biografii i otsenki proizvedenii* (S. Pbg., 1873), pp. 387-88.

[30] Tomashevskii held this in his 1955 article ("Tekst," p. 219), but his 1960 chapter on "Cleopatra" presents the first two lines as a final layer of revision from 1824 (*Pushkin*, II, 55).

Notes: Chapter II

[1] This dating of the revision of "Cleopatra" is based on N. V. Izmailov's account of Pushkin's 1828 manuscripts, "Pushkin v rabote nad 'Poltavoi,'" in *Ocherki tvorchestva Pushkina* (L., 1975), pp. 110-11. Tomashevskii, in 1961, referred to "the fall of 1828" (*Pushkin* [M.-L., 1961], II, 57).

[2] A. A. Akhmatova, *O Pushkine: Stat'i zametki*, ed. È. G. Gershtein (L: Sov. Pis., 1977), pp. 208, 214.

[3] P. A. Viazemskii, as quoted in Pushkin, *Pis'ma*, ed. B. L. Modzalevskii (M.-L., 1928), II, 179.

[4] *Ibid.*, p. 276.

[5] S. Bondi, "K istorii sozdaniia 'Egipetskikh nochei,'" in *Novye stranitsy Pushkina* (M., 1931), p. 151. (See A. L. Vainshtein and V. P. Pavlova, "K istorii povesti Pushkin 'Gosti s'' ezzhalis' na dachu...,'" *Vremennik Pushkinskoii komissii* [1966; pub. L., 1969], pp. 36-43.)

[6] A. P. Kern, *Vospominaniia, dnevniki, perepiska* (M., 1974), p. 30.

[7] Gladkova is surely mistaken when she concludes that Pushkin wanted to introduce the Cleopatra anecdote here. This is a misunderstanding of a purely literary term. Gladkova, p. 309 (see Note 8).

[8] Treatments of the society tale in Pushkin include: E. Gladkova, "Prozaicheskie nabroski Pushkina iz zhizni 'sveta,'" in *Pushkin: Vremennik Pushkinskoi komissii*, vyp. 6 (L., 1941), pp. 305-22; M. A. Belkina, "Svetskaia povest' 30-x godov i 'Kniaginia Ligovskaia' Lermontova," *Zhizn' i tvorchestvo M. Iu. Lermontova: Materialy i issledovaniia*, I (M., 1941), 516-32 ff.; V. Shklovskii, "Svetskaia povest' ('Pikovaia dama'), " in his *Zametki o proze Pushkina* (M.: Sov. Pis., 1937), pp. 53-74; A. V. Chicherin, "Pushkinskie zamysly prozaicheskogo romana," in his *Vozniknovenie romana-èpopei* (M.: Sov. Pis., 1958), pp. 57-

110 ("Guests," pp. 73-80); L. S. Sidiakov, *"Evgenii Onegin* i zamysel 'svetskoi povesti' 30-kh godov XIX v.," *Zamysel, trud, voploshchenie,* ed. V. I. Kuleshov (M.: MGU, 1977), pp. 118-24; N. I. Kolosova, "Antiromanticheskie tendentsii v 'svetskikh' povestiakh i novellakh Pushkina i Merime," *Zhivye traditsii: Iz istorii i teorii literatury* (Saratov, 1978), pp. 42-53.

[9] El'vira Chirpak-Rozdina, "'Egipetskie nochi' A. S. Pushkina," *Studia Slavica,* XIX, fsc. 4 (Budapest, 1973), p. 378.

[10] Quoted in E. A. Baratynskii, *Stikhotvoreniia, poèmy, proza, pis'ma,* ed. K. Pigarev (M., 1951), p. 592.

[11] E. A. Baratynskii, *Stikhotvoreniia i poèmy* (M., 1971), p. 342.

[12] A connection noted without elaboration by M. A. Tsiavlovskii in the notes to A. S. Pushkin, *Polnoe sobranie sochinenii* (L.: Academia, 1936), IV, 762. See also N. N. Petrunina, "Bezzakonnaia kometa" in N. N. Petrunina, G. M. Fridlender, *Nad stranitsami Pushkina* (L.: Nauka, 1974), pp. 43-44.

[13] Petrunina, p. 47.

[14] Osip Mandel'shtam, "Egipetskaia marka," *Sobranie sochinenii,* 2nd ed. (Inter-Language Literary Associates, 1971), II, 24.

[15] Iu. M. Lotman, "Posviashchenie 'Poltavy,'" in *Problemy pushkinovedeniia* (L., 1975), p. 53; N. V. Izmailov, "Pushkin v rabote nad 'Poltavoi,'" in *Ocherki tvorchestva Pushkina* (L., 1975), pp. 64-66.

[16] My analysis is based on the textology of N. V. Izmailov, *ibid.,* primarily pages 39-49, 88-93 and 110-11.

[17] D. D. Blagoi, *Tvorcheskii put' Pushkina (1826-1830)* (M.: Sov. Pis., 1967), p. 324.

[18] Izmailov, p. 91.

[19] Lotman, pp. 48, 51, 53.

[20] Akhmatova, p. 209.

[21] Akhmatova, p. 212.

[22] L. S. Sidiakov has written several informative essays on the relation between the end of *Onegin* and Pushkin's prose of the late 1820's and early 30's. See especially "'Evgenii Onegin' i nezavershennaia proza Pushkina 1828-1830 godov (kharaktery i situatsii)," in *Problemy pushkinovedeniia* (L., 1975), pp. 28-40. Briusov and Veresaev already saw the clear relation between Nina Voronskaya (in Chapter VIII of *Onegin*) and Volskaya/Zakrevskaya. The fact is now a commonplace in commentary to the so-called high society stanzas of Chapter VIII. Sidiakov covers "Guests" on pages 32-39.

[23] Sidiakov, pp. 34-39.

[24] The Jubilee edition dates the fragment to "the end of 1829—the beginning of 1830" and calls its connection with "Guests" of 1828 "problematic" (J. VIII₂, 1050). The ten-volume edition (1964) gives the date as 1830 and says "attributed to the given story by inference [*predpolozhitel'no*] according to the participants in the dialogue, the Spaniard and the Russian" (VI, 788). The textual analysis will make clear the derivation of the later fragment from the earlier. After writing this section, I found one brief discussion of this fragment and its relation to "Egyptian Nights" in N. N. Petrunina, "'Egipetskie nochi' i russkaia povest' 1830-kh godov," *Pushkin: Issledovaniia i materialy,* VIII (1978), 46.

[25] On the prototype of the dacha, see A. L. Vainshtein and V. P. Pavlova, "K istorii povesti Pushkina 'Gosti s' ezzhalis' na dachu...,'" *Vremennik Pushkinskoi komissii* (1966; pub. L., 1969), pp. 36-43.

[26] "Gorod pyshnyi, gorod bednyi," III, 79.

[27] J. III₂, 934-35. See description of the manuscript in N. V. Izmailov, "Osen'," in *Stikhotvoreniia Pushkina 1820-1830-kh godov* (L., 1974), p. 248, n. 62.

[28] Compare Vladimir in "A Novel in Letters": "*Proshedshee dlia nas ne sushchestvuet.... Semeistvennye vospominaniia dvorianstva dolzhny byt' istoricheskimi vospominaniiami naroda*" (VI, 72; 1829).

[29] Madame de Staël, *Dix années d'exil,* édition nouvelle (Paris: Plon, 1904), pp. 330-32. On Madame de Staël and Pushkin see: B. V. Tomashevskii, "'Kinzhal' i Mme de Staël,"

Pushkin i ego sovremenniki, XXXVI (1923), pp. 82-95; B. V. Tomashevskii, *Pushkin i Frantsiia* (L. 1960), index; L. I. Vol'pert, "Pushkin posle vosstaniia dekabristov i kniga Mme de Staël o frantsuzskoi revoliutsii," *Pushkinskii sbornik* (Pskov, 1968), pp. 114-31; L. I. Vol'pert, "Eshche o 'slavnoi shutke' gospozhi de Stal'," *Vremennik Pushkinskoi komissii* (1973; L., pub. 1975), pp. 125-27; P. R. Zaborov, "Zhermena de Stal' i russkaia literatura pervoi treti XIX veka," in *Rannie romanticheskie veianiia*, ed. M. P. Alekseev (L.: Nauka, 1972), pp. 168-203; B. Èdel'shtein, "Zhermena Stal' v prochtenii Pushkina i pushkinskikh geroev," *Trudy* (Goriiskii gos. ped. inst.), XII (Tbilisi, 1968), 133-39.

[30] See L. S. Sidiakov, "Publitsistika v khudozhestvennoi proze Pushkina. (Nezavershennye proizvedeniia rubezha 1830-kh godov i opyt *Evgeniia Onegina*)," *Pushkinskii sbornik*, Uchenye zapiski Leningradskogo gos. ped. inst. imeni Gertsena (Pskov, 1973), pp. 42-59.

[31] P. A. Viazemskii, *Fon-Vizin* (S. Pbg., 1848), pp. 32-33.

[32] See Nikolaus Pevsner and S. Lang, "The Egyptian Revival," *The Architectural Review*, vol. 119, no. 712 (1956), pp. 242-54. For intellectual background see: Erik Iversen, *The Myth of Egypt and its Hieroglyphs* (Copenhagen, 1961).

[33] Russian Egyptiana and Russian Egyptology circa 1830: T. N. Koz'mina-Borozdina, "Razvitie egiptologii v Rossii," *Novyi vostok*, kn. 3 (M., 1923), pp. 342-61; I. S. Katsnel'son, "Materialy po istorii egiptologii v Rossii," *Ocherki po istorii russkogo vostokovedeniia*, II, (M., 1956), pp. 207-32; V. V. Struve, "Peterburgskie sfinksy," *Zapiski klassicheskogo otdeleniia russkogo arkheologicheskogo obshchestva*, VII (S. Pbg., 1913), 20-52; I. G. Livshits, commentary to his edition of Zh.-F. Shampol'on, *O egipetskom alfavite* (L., 1950).

[34] A. A. Formozov, "Pushkin, Chaadaev i Gul'ianov," *Voprosy istorii*, (1966, No. 8), p. 212.

[35] "Neizdannye zametki Anny Akhmatovoi o Pushkine," ed. È. Gershtein, *Voprosy literatury*, (1970, No. 1), p. 191 ("tainopis'").

Notes: Chapter III

[1] The third Cleopatra poem has been discussed, predominantly with a view to establishing its text, by Bondi and then by Tomashevskii. S. Bondi, "K istorii sozdaniia 'Egipetskikh nochei,'" in *Novye stranitsy Pushkina* (M., 1931), pp. 183-88. B. V. Tomashevskii, "Tekst stikhotvoreniia Pushkina 'Kleopatra,'" *Uchenye zapiski LGU*, No. 200, Seriia filologicheskikh nauk, vyp. 25 (1955), pp. 220-23. See also B. V. Tomashevskii, "Kleopatra," in *Pushkin* (M.-L., 1961), II, 59-65.

[2] Tomashevskii, "Tekst," p. 223.

[3] Bondi, "K istorii," p. 183.

[4] The ten-volume edition now prints it as a footnote to the text of the 1828 poem. The editors were not convinced by Tomashevskii's arguments that this verse segment belongs at the beginning and not the end.

[5] Tomashevskii, "Tekst," p. 222.

[6] Tomashevskii, *Pushkin*, II, 59, 60, 63-64; "Tekst," p. 223.

[7] W. Lednicki, "Pochemu Pushkin ne okonchil 'Egipetskie nochi,'" *Novyi zhurnal*, 90-91 (1968), 244-55.

[8] Lednicki, p. 250. On page 251, Lednicki identifies "Le Comte de St. Germain," which is Chapter XXXIII in the edition available to me, as Chapter XXX. He also refers rather mysteriously to "a fragment of the same Janin, 'A Night in Alexandria,'" which I have been unable to identify.

[9] Jules Janin, Barnave, réimprimé sur l'édition originelle (Paris, 1878), p. 308.

[10] Jules de Saint Félix, *Cléopâtre: Reine d'Égypte* (Brussels and Leipzig, 1855), pp. 7-8.

[11] Tomashevskii has established that Pushkin was using Shakespeare, in French translation, and not Plutarch directly in the case of the barque scene (Tomashevskii, *Pushkin*, II, 61).

[12]Heinrich Heine, *Werke und Briefe* (Berlin, 1961), V, 493-500.

[13]V. Ia. Briusov, "Egipetskie nochi," *Moi Pushkin*, (M.-L., 1929), p. 112. See the critique of Briusov in I. Nusinov, *"Antonii i Kleopatra* Shekspira i 'Egipetskie nochi' Pushkina," *Pushkin i mirovaia literatura* (M., 1941), pp. 321-26.

[14]Noted by Bondi, "K istorii," p. 179.

[15]J. VIII₂, 1061. Cf. ten-volume edition, VI, 800: "probably in 1835, before 'Egyptian Nights.'"

[16]VI, 801: "begun in November, 1833, but Pushkin continued to work on it in 1835 as well; the verse fragments belonging with it date to 1835." Cf. J. VIII₂, 1057.

[17]The literature on "A Tale from Roman Life" is limited. Bondi did not consider it to be a part of the history of the cycle ("K istorii," p. 151). P. V. Annenkov did discuss it in this light (*A. S. Pushkin: Materialy dlia ego biografii i otsenki proizvedenii*, [S. Pbg., 1873], pp. 387-93); however, many of these few pages are taken up with reproduction of the text. N. I. Cherniaev wrote an interesting and informative essay on the story in his *Kriticheskie stat'i i zametki o Pushkine* (Khar'kov, 1900), pp. 422-87, but without comprehensive reference to the history of the cycle.

[18]Cherniaev, pp. 481-82.

[19]Cherniaev, p. 441.

[20]Tacitus, *Annals*, Book 16, Chs. 18-19.

[21]Anna Akhmatova, *O Pushkine: Stat'i i zametki*, ed. È. G. Gershtein (L.: Sov. Pis., 1977), p. 205.

[22]As established by G. Gel'd, "Pushkin i Afinei," *Pushkin i ego sovremenniki*, XXXI-XXXII (L., 1927), pp. 15-18; and M. P. Alekseev, "K istorii 'Podrazhanii drevnim' Pushkina," *Vremennik Pushkinskoi komissii* (1962; L., pub. 1963), pp. 20-29.

[23]A. Malein, "Pushkin, Avrelii Viktor i Tatsit," *Pushkin v mirovoi literature* (L., 1929), pp. 11-12.

[24]For contemporary descriptions of Briullov's painting, see N. G. Mashkovtsev, ed., *K. P. Briullov v pis'makh, dokumentakh i vospominaniiakh sovremennikov* (M., 1961), pp. 76-111.

[25]V. È. Vatsuro, "'K Vel'mozhe,'" in the collection *Stikhotvoreniia Pushkina 1820-1830-kh godov* (L., 1974), p. 211.

[26]There is a difference, of course, between Juvenal and Petronius. In the words of Nisard, whose book Pushkin counted in his library:

> Je trouve que sous le cynisme effronté de Pétrone, sous sa gaîté libertine, il y a plus de colère réelle et plus d'arrières-pensées courageuses que sous l'austère pédanterie de Juvénal. C'est peut-être pour cela que Pétrone conspira contre Néron, et s'ouvrit les veines, au lieu que Juvénal ne conspira contre personne, et mourut dans son lit.

D. Nisard, *Etudes de moeurs et de critique sur les poètes latins de la décadence* (Paris, 1834), I, 456-57.

[27]P. V. Annenkov, *A. S. Pushkin: Materialy dlia ego biografii i otsenki proizvedenii* (S. Pbg., 1873), p. 388. See Ushakov, *Tolkovyi slovar' russkogo iazyka: "Romanicheskii"*—(1) pertaining to fiction, like the plot of a novel; (2) romantic interest, romantic/erotic.

[28]Akhmatova was interested in the connections between the two fragments but never was able to elaborate on them (Akhmatova, pp. 181-82).

[29]Vershnev, the archive youth, is perhaps the foil in "Evening at the Dacha." He has the attraction to speculative philosophy of the youth in "A Tale from Roman Life" without his appealing naivete. At one point in the draft Pushkin refers to him as *"iunosha Vershnev"* (J. VIII₂, 991).

[30]Akhmatova, p. 197.

[31]Precisely at this juncture the manuscript changes from fair copy to rough draft (J. VIII₂, 1061).

[32]Akhmatova, p. 179.

[33]See note 7 above.

[34]V. È. Vatsuro, "'K Vel'mozhe,'" in *Stikhotvoreniia Pushkina 1820-1830-kh godov* (L., 1974), p. 211.

[35]Lednicki, p. 254.

[36]B. V. Tomashevskii, *Pushkin i Frantsiia* (L., 1960), pp. 392-95. The angle of Pushkin's ideological interest in *Barnave* remains to be defined. Tomashevskii simply remarks, "the socio-political conception of the French revolutionary movement is very close to Pushkin's views" (p. 393). As a political novel *Barnave* was directed against the new bourgeois dynasty and showed the chaos of contemporary society where the old values had been shattered by revolution.

[37]On the role of the anecdote in Pushkin's prose fiction, see L. P. Grossman, "Iskusstvo anekdota u Pushkina," and "Ustnaia novella Pushkina" in his *Etiudy o Pushkine* (M.-Pgd., 1923), pp. 37-77, 77-115. He discusses the "Egyptian Nights" cycle on pages 46, 63, 68-69. As Grossman would agree, Pushkin's method, although based on anecdote, is not anecdote pure and simple. Nevertheless, Grossman has a tendency to leave aside the analytical Pushkin who is not just a *conteur*.

[38]William Hazlitt, "On the Fear of Death," *Table-Talk* (Paris, 1825), II, 19 (final words of quotation supplied from p. 20). Page 19 is one of the pages marked in the copy from Pushkin's library, according to B. Modzalevskii, "Biblioteka Pushkina," *Pushkin i ego sovremenniki*, vyp. IX-X (S. Pbg., 1910), p. 246.

[39]Bondi, though he spoke of parody, assumed repetition of the Cleopatra anecdote ("K istorii," p. 179). So did Akhmatova, who considered "Evening at the Dacha" to be a prose fragment complete in itself and would have liked to have seen it dated later than "Egyptian Nights" (Akhmatova, pp. 197-98). Annenkov and Tomashevskii, on the other hand, and even Briusov, believed that Pushkin's treatment would end differently. For Annenkov, see note 27 above. Tomashevskii, *Pushkin*, II, 64, note; Briusov, p. 118. I. M. Toibin has tried to settle the question definitively by arguing Pushkin's negative attitude toward the cyclical theories of history which were current in the 1830's. See his "Voprosy istorizma i khudozhestvennaia sistema Pushkina 1830-kh godov," *Pushkin: Issledovaniia i materialy*, VI (L., 1969), 43-44. I was unable to consult Toibin's article "'Egipetskie nochi' i nekotorye voprosy tvorchestva Pushkina 1830-ch godov," *Uch. zap. Orlovskogo ped. inst.*, 30 (1966), 112-52.

[40]Madame de Staël, *Dix années d'exil*, Ch. XIX (Paris, 1904), p. 364.

[41]Tomashevskii, *Pushkin*, II, 64, note.

[42]Anna Akhmatova, "Neizdannye zapiski Anny Akhmatovoi o Pushkine," ed. È. Gershtein, *Voprosy literatury*, (1970, No. 1), p. 191. This fragment was not reprinted in the 1977 book.

[43]*Ibid.*, 192.

[44]*Ibid.*, 206.

Notes: Chapter IV

[1]Ralph E. Matlaw, "Poetry and the Poet in Romantic Society as Reflected in Pushkin's 'Egyptian Nights,'" *Slavonic and East European Review*, Vol. 33, No. 80 (1954), 102.

[2]L. S. Sidiakov, "K izucheniiu 'Egipetskikh nochei,'" *Pushkin: Issledovaniia i materialy*, IV (M.-L., 1962), 173, 178.

[3]L. Ginzburg, "Pushkin i liricheskii geroi russkogo romantizma," *Pushkin: Issledovaniia i materialy*, IV (M.-L., 1962), 140-54. Wiktor Weintraub, "The Problem of Improvisation in Romantic Literature," *Comparative Literature*, XVI (1964), 131-37 (on "Egyptian Nights").

[4]Most clearly stated by L. Rzhevskii, "Strukturnaia tema 'Egipetskikh nochei,'" in *Alexander Pushkin: A Symposium on the 175th Anniversary of his Death*, Andrej Kodjak and Kiril Taranovsky, eds., N. Y. Univ. Slavic Papers, Vol. I (New York: N. Y. Univ. Press, 1976), pp. 126-35.

[5]See V. Briusov, "Egipetskie nochi," in *Moi Pushkin* (M.-L., 1929), pp. 107-18; and Matlaw, pp. 112-17.

[6]Anna Akhmatova, *O Pushkine: Stat'i i zametki*, ed. È. G. Gershtein (L., 1977), p. 169.

[7]Madame de Staël, *Oeuvres complètes* (Paris, 1820), IX, 107. The bookmark is recorded in B. Modzalevskii, "Biblioteka Pushkina," *Pushkin i ego sovremenniki*, vyp. IX-X (S. Pbg., 1910), p. 342.

[8]Konstantin Èrburg, *Tsel' tvorchestva: Opyty po teorii tvorchestva i èstetike* (M., 1913), p. 126.

[9]D. N. Ovsianiko-Kulikovskii, *Sobranie sochinenii* (S. Pbg., 1911), IV, *Pushkin*, 149-53.

[10]Thus, in the 1920's, speculation even ranged on the possibility of interpreting "Egyptian Nights" as a disguised representation of the Decembrist uprising. See L. N. Voitolovskii, "Pushkin i ego sovremennost'," *Krasnaia nov'*, (1925, No. 6), pp. 246-59.

[11]This interpretation is shared by W. Lednicki and M. Gorlin. See M. Gorlin, "'Noce egipskie'(Kompozycja i Geneza)," in *Puszkin*, ed. W. Lednicki (Krakow, 1939), I, 128-45. Rpt. in Michael Gorlin and R. Bloch-Gorlina, *Études littéraires et historiques* (Paris: Institut d'Études slaves, 1957), pp. 137-57. W. Lednicki, "Pochemu Pushkin ne okonchil 'Egipetskie nochi,'" *Novyi zhurnal*, 90-91 (1968), 244-55.

[12]I. Nusinov, "'Antonii i Kleopatra' Shekspira i 'Egipetskie nochi' Pushkina," *Pushkin i mirovaia literatura* (M., 1941), p. 327. See also Matlaw, p. 119.

[13]VI, 589. Although "A Fragment" was not originally connected with the Cleopatra material, to exclude it completely from the creative history of "Egyptian Nights," as Bondi wished, seems unjustified. S. M. Bondi, "K istorii sozdaniia 'Egipetskikh nocheii,'" *Novye stranitsy Pushkina* (M., 1931), p. 198.

[14]See Ginzburg. On the creative history of the first improvisation see O. S. Solov'eva, "'Ezerskii' i 'Mednyi vsadnik,' Istoriia teksta," *Pushkin: Issledovaniia i materialy*, III (M.-L., 1960), 333-34, 338-39. The improvisation adapts a digression in "Ezerskii" which was originally intended as an apology for the "low," modern tale that forms Part Two of *The Bronze Horseman*.

[15]Blok: "Khot' vse po prezhnemu *pevets*... No k tseli blizitsia *poèt*... " (emphasis Blok's), *Ante lucem*, "Khot' vse po prezhnemu *pevets*," 1900. In Blok's case, the "singer" seems to refer to a poet of Fet's type.

[16]The latest treatment of the relation of these poems to "Egyptian Nights" along with a list of earlier references will be found in Sidiakov. I have deliberately omitted to discuss the question of real prototypes for the improvisor. Interested readers should consult my bibliography under Kazanovich and Lednicki's article on Mickiewicz and Pushkin (pp. 69-82). Akhmatova was also given to the direct biographical approach (pp. 192-97 and elsewhere). Much more interesting are Ginzburg and Petrunina on the literary models available in Russia for the romantic artist, of which the Italian improvisor was one variant. (N. N. Petrunina, "'Egipetskie nochi' i russkaia povest' 1830-kh godov," *Pushkin: Issledovaniia i materialy*, VIII [L., 1978], 22-50.)

[17]V. Vinogradov, "Khudozhestvennoe myshlenie literaturnymi stiliami," in *Stil' Pushkina* (M., 1941), pp. 480-513; and, in particular, S. G. Bocharov, "Stilisticheskii mir romana ('Evgenii Onegin')," *Poètika Pushkina* (M., 1974), pp. 26-105. See also G. A. Gukovksii on the nature of Pushkin's stylizations in *Pushkin i problemy realisticheskogo stilia* (M. 1957), p. 109ff. This is something akin to Bakhtin's notion of *obraz stilia*.

[18]Weintraub, p. 137; vs. Lednicki, p. 248 (following Gorlin).

[19]This distinction underlies, for instance, N. Mandel'shtam's discussion of the poet and the improvisor in her essay "Motsart i Sal'eri," *Vestnik russkogo khristianskogo dvizheniia* (Paris-New York, June, 1972); *Mozart and Salieri*, tr. Robert A. McLean (Ann Arbor: Ardis, 1973).

[20]The title of Ginzburg's article.

[21]See, for example, Sidiakov, pp. 175-76.

[22]Akhmatova, p. 197.

[23]Ginzburg, p. 150. The suggestion about the particular passage was first made by Nusinov, p. 345. The commentator who wrote the entry for "Egyptian Nights" in *Putevoditel' po Pushkinu* sensed its typological similarity with Heine's Hoffmannesque tale bearing the remarkably similar title "Florentinische Nächte" which features the mysterious virtuoso Paganini. A much-edited version came out in 1836, the authentic text not until 1837. Pushkin would probably have waited for the French translation.

[24]I cannot agree with Tomashevskii that the themes are merely the literary fashion and trite (commentaries: VI, 777-78).

[25]See the introduction to S. M. Bondi's article, "Iz 'Poslednei tetradi' Pushkina," in the collection *Stikhotvoreniia Pushkina 1820-30-kh godov* (L., 1974), pp. 377-79.

[26]See Jubilee edition, notes to "A Tale from Roman Life," J. VIII₂, 1061.

[27]J. VIII₂, 1061.

[28]See Tomashevskii, "Tekst," p. 220.

[29]See S. M. Bondi, "Iz 'Poslednei tetradi' Pushkina," p. 384. The best sense of what is going forward in Pushkin's notebooks in 1835 is found in Bondi's article, pp. 382-84. I have relied on it, checking as many dates as possible with the ten-volume edition.

[30]Briusov, p. 116. The title of the book is from Modzalevskii's catalogue of Pushkin's library (see reference in Note 7 above).

[31]Akhmatova, pp. 205-06.

[32]N. N. Petrunina has conjectured that certain reflections in the first improvisation ("*Poèt idet—otkryty vezhdy*") are connected with a pause in work on "Na vyzdorovlenie Lukulla." See her article "'Na vyzdorovlenie Lukulla,'" in *Stikhotvoreniia Pushkina 1820-1830-kh godov* (L., 1974), p. 346.

[33]See I. Feinberg's treatment of this category in his book *Nezavershennye raboty Pushkina*, 4th ed. (M., 1964), p. 319.

[34]P. Viazemskii, tr., *Adol'f: Roman Benzhamen-Konstana* (S. Pbg., 1831), xv.

Notes: Conclusion

[1]A. A. Akhmatova, *O Pushkine: Stat'i i zametki*, ed. È. G. Gershtein (L.: Sov. Pis., 1977), p. 200.

[2]P. V. Annenkov, *A. S. Pushkin: Materialy dila ego biografii i otsenki proizvedenii* (S. Pbg., 1873), p. 414.

[3]Iu. Tynianov, "Pushkin," in his *Pushkin i ego sovremenniki* (M., 1969), pp. 122-23.

[4]A. A. Akhmatova, p. 192. "*Pushkinskaia proza—otstoiavshaiasia.*"

[5]S. G. Bocharov, "Poèticheskoe predanie i poètika Pushkina," in the collection *Pushkin i literatura narodov Sovetskogo Soiuza* (Erevan, 1975), pp. 54-74.

[6]S. G. Bocharov (after Veselovskii) in his *Poètika Pushkina* (M., 1974), p. 56.

[7]See *Bibliografiia proizvedenii A. S. Pushkina i literatury o nem, 1918-1936*, Chast' II (L., 1973) and additional volumes for later years in series, index under "Egyptian Nights."

[8]O. È. Mandel'shtam, *Sobranie sochinenii*, 2nd ed. (New York: Inter-Language Literary Associates, 1971), II, 9-10; 283.

[9]Mandel'shtam, I (1967), 159.

[10]Mandel'shtam, II, 38. As translated by Clarence Brown, in *The Prose of Osip Mandelstam* (Princeton: Princeton Univ. Press, 1965), pp. 184-85.

[11]V. V. Khlebnikov, *Sobranie sochinenii* (L., 1928-33; rpt. Munich: Fink, 1968), II (Vols. 3-4 of orig. ed.), 2nd pagination, p. 333n.

[12]A. A. Blok, *Sobranie sochinenii* (M.: Biblioteka "Ogonek," 1971), II, 172-73.

[13]Blok, V, 335-36.

[14]A. A. Akhmatova, *Sochineniia*, 2nd ed. (New York: Inter-Language Literary Associates, 1967), I, 238.

SELECTED BIBLIOGRAPHY

Akhmatova, Anna A. "Neizdannye zametki Anny Akhmatovoi o Pushkine." Ed. È. Gershtein. *Voprosy literatury*, 1970, No. 1, pp. 158-206. Reprinted, revised, some omissions, in Anna Akhmatova, *O Pushkine: Stat'i i zametki.* Ed. È. G. Gershtein. L.: Sov. Pis., 1977, pp. 161-72, 174-223.

Annenkov, Pavel V. *A. S. Pushkin: Materialy dlia ego biografii i otsenki proizvedenii.* S. Pbg.: 1873, pp. 387-93.

Bagdasariants, Ia. K. "K istorii teksta 'Egipetskikh nochei.'" In *Pushkin: Stat'i i materialy.* Ed. M. P. Alekseev. II. Odessa: Odesskii dom uchenykh, 1926, pp. 88-91.

Belkina, M. A. "Svetskaia povest' 30-kh godov i 'Kniaginia Ligovskaia' Lermontova." In *Zhizn' i tvorchestvo M. Iu. Lermontova: Materialy i issledovaniia.* Ed. N. L. Brodskii. M.: 1941, I, pp. 516-32 ff.

Bibliografiia proizvedenii A. S. Pushkina i literatury o nem: 1918-1936. Ed. Ia. L. Levkovich. L.: Nauka, 1973, Chast' II, index under "Egyptian Nights." See also later volumes in this series.

Bondi, Sergei M. "K istorii sozdaniia 'Egipetskikh nochei.'" In his *Novye stranitsy Pushkina.* M.: Mir, 1931, pp. 148-205.

Briusov, Valerii Ia. "Egipetskie nochi." In his *Moi Pushkin.* M.-L.: Gos. izd., 1929, pp. 107-18. Originally published in *Sochineniia Pushkina,* IV. Ed. S. A. Vengerov. S. Pbg.: 1910, pp. 444-449.

Cherniaev, N. I. "'Tsezar' puteshestvoval' (Otryvok o smerti Petroniia)." In his *Kriticheskie stat'i i zametki o Pushkine.* Kharkov: 1900, pp. 422-86.

Chicherin, Boris. "Pushkinskie zamysly prozaicheskogo romana." In his *Vozniknovenie romana-èpopei.* M.: Sov. Pis., 1958, pp. 57-110.

Chirpak-Rozdina, El'vira. "'Egipetskie nochi' A. S. Pushkina." *Studia Slavica,* T. 19, Fascicle 4 (Budapest, 1973), pp. 373-90.

Debreczeny, Paul. *The Other Pushkin: A Study of Alexander Pushkin's Prose Fiction.* Stanford: Stanford Univ. Press, 1983, pp. 41-51, 282-98.

Dostoevskii, F. M. "Otvet *Russkomu vestniku*" in his *Polnoe sobranie sochinenii v tridtsati tomakh.* Vol. 19. L.: Nauka, 1979, pp. 119-39 (first published 1861).

Garibian, D. A. "Nekotorye stilisticheskie nabliudeniia nad tekstami 'Egipetskikh nochei' Pushkina i Briusova." In *Briusovskie chteniia 1962 goda.* Erevan: Armianskoe gos. izd., 1963, pp. 232-45.

Ginzburg, Lidia Ia. "Pushkin i liricheskii geroi russkogo romantizma." *Pushkin: Issledovaniia i materialy.* IV (M.-L.: Nauka, 1962), pp. 140-54.

Gladkova, Elena. "Proizaicheskie nabroski Pushkina iz zhizni 'sveta.'" *Pushkin: Vremennik Pushkinkoi komissii,* vyp. 6 (L., 1941), pp. 305-22.

Gofman (Hofman), Modest L. *Egipetskie nochi: s polnym tekstom improvizatsii Italiantsa, s novoi, chetvertoi glavoi—Pushkina i s Prilozheniem (zakliuchitel'naia piataia glava).* Paris: Serge Lifar, 1935.

————. "'Les Nuits Égyptiennes' de Pouchkine et leur héroine." *Le Monde slave,* 1933, No. 4, pp. 346-59.

Gorlin, Michael. "'Noce egipskie' (Kompozycja i Geneza)." In *Puszkin.* Ed. Waclaw Lednicki. Vol. I. Krakow: 1939, pp. 128-45. Rpt. in Michael Gorlin and R. Block-Gorlina. *Études littéraires et historiques.* Paris: Institut d'Études slaves, 1957, pp. 137-57.

Gornaia, V. "Iz nabluidenii nad stilem romana *Anna Karenina*: O pushkinskikh tradistiiakh v romane." *Tolstoi-khudozhnik: Sbornik statei.* Ed. D. D. Blagoi. M., 1961, pp. 181-206.

Gorokhova, R. M. "K tekstu 'Egipetskikh nochei.'" *Pushkin: Vremennik Pushkinskoi komissii* (1966; pub. L., 1969), pp. 49-50.

Iakovlev, N. V. "Iz razyskanii o literaturnykh istochnikakh v tvorchestve Pushkina. III. Pushkin i Kol'dridzh." In Iakovlev, ed., *Pushkin v mirovoi literature*. L.: Gos. izd., 1926, pp. 137-45.

Kazanovich, E. "K istochnikam 'Egipetskikh nochei.'" *Zven'ia*, III-IV (M.-L., 1934), pp. 187-204.

Khodasevich, V. "Knigi i liudi: 'Egipetskie nochi.'" *Vozrozhdenie*. Vol. 13, No. 12 (1934).

Kirpotin, Valerii Ia. "Dostoevskii o 'Egipetskikh nochakh' Pushkina." *Voprosy literatury*, 1962, No. 11, pp. 112-22.

Komarovich, Vasilii L. "Dostoevskii i 'Egipetskie nochi' Pushkina." *Pushkin i ego sovremenniki*, XXIX-XXX (1918), pp. 36-48.

Lednicki, Waclaw. "Pochemu Pushkin ne okonchil 'Egipetskie nochi.'" *Novyi zhurnal*, 90-91 (1968), 244-55.

———. "Mickiewicz's Stay in Russia and his Friendship with Pushkin." In *Adam Mickiewicz and World Literature: A Symposium*. Ed. W. Lednicki. Berekeley: Univ. of Calif. Press, 1956, pp. 13-104 ("Egyptian Nights," pp. 69-82).

Mandel'shtam, Nadezhda. *Mozart and Salieri*. Tr. Robert A. McLean. Ann Arbor: Ardis, 1973. (Nadezhda Mandel'shtam. "Motsart i Sal'eri." *Vestnik russkogo khristianskogo dvizheniia*. Paris-New York, June, 1972.)

Matlaw, Ralph E. "Poetry and the Poet in Romantic Society as Reflected in Pushkin's *Egyptian Nights*." *Slavonic and East European Review*, Vol. 33, No. 80 (1954), pp. 102-19.

Novitskii, Pavel I. "'Egipetskie nochi' Pushkina." In A. S. Pushkin, *Egipetskie nochi*, L.: Academia, 1927, pp. 37-81.

Nusinov, Isaak. "'Antonii i Kleopatra' Shekspira i 'Egipetskie nochi' Pushkina." *Pushkin i mirovaia literatura*. M.: Sov. Pis., 1941, pp. 285-345.

Odinokov, V. G. "'Egipetskie nochi' A. S. Pushkina v protsesse 'ukrupneniia zhanra.'" *Khudozhestvennoe tvorchestvo i literaturnyi protsess*. Tomsk: Izd. Tomskogo univ., 1 (1976), 26-33.

Ovsianiko-Kulikovskii, Dmitrii N. *Sobranie sochinenii*. IV. *Pushkin*. S. Pbg.: 1911, pp. 139-60.

Petrunina, N. N. "'Egipetskie nochi' i russkaia povest' 1830-kh godov." *Pushkin: Issledovaniia i materialy*, VIII (L.: Nauka, 1978), pp. 22-50.

Praz, Mario. *The Romantic Agony*. 2nd ed. London: Oxford Univ. Press. "La Belle Dame sans merci," especially pp. 213-16.

Rzhevskii, Leonid. "Strukturnaia tema 'Egipetskikh nochei.'" In *Alexander Pushkin: A Symposium on the 175th Anniversary of his Birth*. New York Univ. Slavonic Papers, Vol. 1. Andrej Kodjak and Kiril Taranovsky, eds. New York: New York Univ. Press, 1976, pp. 126-35.

Shaginian, R. and I. Syrtsov. "O dialogicheski-kontrapunkticheskom stroenii 'Egipetskikh nochei' (K probleme: Pushkin i Dostoevskii)." *Filologicheskie i pedagogicheskie nauki*. Samarkand, 1977, pp. 28-39.

Shervinskii, Sergei V. "Iz 'Egipetskikh nochei.'" In his *Ritm i smysl*. M.: Nauka, 1961, pp. 137-56.

Sidiakov, L. S. "K izucheniiu 'Egipetskikh nochei.'" *Pushkin: Issledovaniia i materialy*, IV (M.-L.: Nauka, 1962), pp. 173-82.

———. *Khudozhestvennaia proza A. S. Pushkina*. Riga: LGU im. Petra Stuchki, 1973, pp. 51-56 ("Guests"), pp. 136-148 ("Egyptian Nights").

———. "'Evgenii Onegin' i nezavershennaia proza Pushkina 1828-1830 godov (kharaktery i situatsii)." In *Problemy pushkinovedeniia*. L.: L. gos. ped. inst. im. Gertsena, 1975, pp. 28-40.

Toibin, I. M. "'Egipetskie nochi' i nekotorye voprosy tvorchestva Pushkina 1830-kh godov." *Uchenye zapiski Orlovskogo pedagogicheskogo instituta*, 30 (1966), 112-52.

Tomashevskii, Boris V. "Tekst stikhotvoreniia Pushkina 'Kleopatra.'" *Uchenye zapiski LGU*, No. 200 (1955), Seriia filologicheskikh nauk, vyp. 25, p. 216-29.

———. *Pushkin*. M.-L.: 1961. II, 55-65.

Vainshtein, A. L., and V. P. Pavlova. "K istorii povesti Pushkina 'Gosti s"ezzhalis' na dachu...'" *Vremennik Pushkinskoi komissii* (1966; publ. L., 1969), pp. 36-43.

142

Val'be, B. "'Egipetskie nochi,'" *Zvezda* (1937), No. 3, pp. 143-57.

Vodovozov, N. V. "Neokonchennaia povest' Pushkina." *Uch. zap. Mosk. gos. ped. inst. im. Potemkina.* Vol. 94, No. 8 (1959), 71-104.

Voitolovskii, Lev N. "Pushkin i ego sovremennost'." *Krasnaia nov'* (1925), No. 6, pp. 228-59 ("Egipetskie nochi," pp. 246ff.).

Weintraub, Wiktor. "The Problem of Improvisation in Romantic Literature." *Comparative Literature*, XVI (1964), 119-37.

Zhirmunskii, Viktor. "'Egipetskie nochi' Valeriia Briusova." In his *Valerii Briusov i nasledie Pushkina.* Petrograd: Èl'zevir, 1922, pp. 52-94. Rpt. V. M. Zhirmunskii, *Izbrannye trudy.* L., Nauka: 1977, pp. 142-205.

APPENDIX

Below is Pushkin's Russian for the poems quoted in English translation. They are referenced to the appropriate page.

1. Пушкин, „Клеопатра" (1824) (pp. 11-13).

Царица голосом и взором
Свой пышный оживляла пир,
Все, Клеопатру славя хором,
В ней признавали свой кумир,
Шумя, текли к ее престолу,
Но вдруг над чашей золотой
Она задумалась — и долу
Поникла дивною главой.

И пышный пир как будто дремлет,
И в ожиданье все молчит. . .
Но вновь она чело подъемлет
И с видом важным говорит:
„Внемлите мне: могу равенство
Меж вас и мной восстановить.
В моей любви для вас блаженство,
Блаженство можно вам купить:
Кто к торгу страстному приступит?
Свои я ночи продаю.
Скажите, кто меж вами купит
Ценою жизни ночь мою?"

Она рекла. Толпа в молчанье,
И всех в волнении сердца.
Но Клеопатра в ожиданье
С холодной дерзостью лица:
„Я жду, — вещает, — что ж молчите?
Иль вы теперь бежите прочь?
Вас было много; приступите,
Торгуйте радостную ночь."

И гордый взор она обводит
Кругом поклонников своих. . .
Вдруг — из рядов один выходит,
Вослед за ним и два других.

Смела их поступь, ясны очи.
Царица гордо восстает.
Свершилось: куплены три ночи...
И ложе смерти их зовет.

И снова гордый глас возвысила царица:
„Забыты мною днесь венец и багряница!
Простой наемницей на ложе восхожу;
Неслыханно тебе, Киприда, я служу,
И новый дар тебе ночей моих награда,
О боги грозные, внемлите ж, боги ада,
Подземных ужасов печальные цари!
Примите мой обет: до сладостной зари
Властителей моих последние желанья
И дивной негою и тайнами лобзанья,
Всей чашею любви послушно упою...
Но только сквозь завес во храмину мою
Блеснет Авроры луч — клянусь моей порфирой, —
Главы их упадут под утренней секирой!"

Благословенные священною рукой,
Из урны жребии выходят чередой,
И первый Аквила, клеврет Помпея смелый,
Изрубленный в боях, в походах поседелый.
Презренья хладного не снес он от жены
И гордо выступил, суровый сын войны,
На вызов роковых последних наслаждений,
Как прежде выступал на славный клик сражений.
Критон за ним, Критон, изнеженный мудрец,
Воспитанный под небом Арголиды,
От самых первых дней поклонник и певец
И пламенных пиров и пламенной Киприды.
Последний имени веками не передал,
Никем не знаемый, ничем не знаменитый;
Чуть отроческий пух, темнея, покрывал
Его стыдливые ланиты.
Огонь любви в очах его пылал,
Во всех чертах любовь изображалась —
Он Клеопатрою, казалося, дышал,
И молча долго им царица любовалась.

(II, 222-24)

2. Пушкин, „Клеопатра" (р. 17).

Но вдруг над чашей золотой
Она задумалась — и долу
Поникла дивною главой.

        И пышный пир как будто дремлет,
И в ожиданье все молчит. . .
Но вновь она чело подъемлет
И с видом важным говорит. . .

    Пушкин, „Бахчисарайский фонтан"

Гирей сидел, потупя взор;
Янтарь в устах его дымился;
Безмолвно раболепный двор
Вкруг хана грозного теснился.
Все было тихо во дворце;
Благоговея, все читали
Приметы гнева и печали
На сумрачном его лице. . .

Живее строгое чело
Волненье сердца выражает. . .

        Что движет гордою душою?
Какою мыслью занят он?

(IV, 177)

3. Пушкин, „Евгений Онегин" (р. 18).

А ложа, где, красой блистая,
Негоциантка молодая,
Самолюбива и томна,
Толпой рабов окружена?
Она и внемлет и не внемлет
И каватине, и мольбам,
И шутке с лестью пополам. . .
А муж — в углу за нею дремлет. . .

(V, 208)

4. Пушкин, 1826

Тебя уж нет, о ты, которой
Я в бурях жизни молодой
Обязан опытом ужасным
И рая мигом сладострастным.

(V, 538, Ch. VI, variants)

5. Пушкин, „Прозерпина" (pp. 19-20).

Плещут волны Флегетона,
Своды тартара дрожат:
Кони бледного Плутона
Быстро к нимфам Пелиона
Из аида бога мчат.
Вдоль пустынного залива
Прозерпина вслед за ним,
Равнодушна и ревнива,
Потекла путем одним.
Пред богинею колена
Робко юноша склонил.
И богиням льстит измена:
Прозерпине смертный мил.
Ада гордая царица
Взором юношу зовет,
Обняла, и колесница
Уж к аиду их несет:
Мчатся, облаком одеты;
Видят вечные луга,
Элизей и томной Леты
Усыпленные брега.
Там бесмертье, там забвенье,
Там утехам нет конца.
Прозерпина в упоенье,
Без порфиры и венца,
Повинуется желаньям,
Предает его лобзаньям
Сокровенные красы,
В сладострастной неге тонет
И молчит и томно стонет...
Но бегут любви часы;
Плещут волны Флегетона,

Своды тартара дрожат:
Кони бледного Плутона
Быстро мчат его назад.
И Кереры дочь уходит,
И счастливца за собой
Из Элизия выводит
Потаенною тропой;
И счастливец отпирает
Осторожною рукой
Дверь, откуда вылетает
Сновидений ложный рой.

(II, 179-80, emphasis added)

6. Пушкин, ,,Жених" (p. 21).

Вот и жених — и все за стол,
    Звенят, гремят стаканы,
Заздравный ковш кругом пошел;
    Все шумно, гости пьяны.

            Жених

,,А что же, милые друзья,
Невеста красная моя
    Не пьет, не ест, не служит:
    О чем невеста тужит?"

7. Пушкин, 1824 (p. 22).

Недвижный страж дремал на царственном пороге,
Владыка севера один в своем чертоге
Безмолвно бодрствовал, и жребии земли
В увенчанной главе стесненные лежали,
            Чредою выпадали
И миру тихую неволю в дар несли, —
.   .   .   .   .   .
,,Свершилось! — молвил он. . .
    Раздался бой полночи —
И се внезапный гость в чертог царя предстал.

(II, 175-76: 1824)

149

8. Пушкин, „Клеопатра", 1824 (р. 23).

Мне жаль великия жены,
Жены, которая любила
Все роды славы: дым войны
И дым парнасского кадила.

.   .   .   .   .   .

Старушка милая жила
Приятно и немного блудно. . .
(II, 231)

9. Пушкин, „Евгений Онегин" (р. 23).

Онегин полетел к театру,
Где каждый, вольностью дыша,
Готов охлопать *entrechat,*
Обшикать Федру, Клеопатру. . .
(I, 17)

10. Пушкин, „Клеопатра", 1828 (рр. 24-26).

Чертог сиял. Гремели хором
Певцы при звуке флейт и лир.
Царица голосом и взором
Свой пышный оживляла пир;
Сердца неслись к ее престолу,
Но вдруг над чашей золотой
Она задумалась и долу
Поникла дивною главой...

И пышный пир как будто дремлет,
Безмолвны гости. Хор молчит.
Но вновь она чело подъемлет
И с видом ясным говорит:
В моей любви для вас блаженство?
Блаженство можно вам купить...
Внемлите ж мне: могу равенство
Меж нами я восстановить.

Кто к торгу страстному приступит?
Свою любовь я продаю;
Скажите: кто меж вами купит
Ценою жизни ночь мою? —

— Клянусь... — о матерь наслаждений,
Тебе неслыханно служу,
На ложе страстных искушений
Простой наемницей всхожу.
Внемли же, мощная Киприда,
И вы, подземные цари,
О боги грозного Аида,
Клянусь — до утренней зари
Моих властителей желанья
Я сладострастно утомлю
И всеми тайнами лобзанья
И дивной негой утолю.
Но только утренней порфирой
Аврора вечная блеснет,
Клянусь — под смертною секирой
Глава счастливцев отпадет.

Рекла — и ужас всех объемлет,
И страстью дрогнули сердца...
Она смущенный ропот внемлет
С холодной дерзостью лица,
И взор презрительный обводит
Кругом поклонников своих...
Вдруг из толпы один выходит,
Вослед за ним и два других.
Смела их поступь; ясны очи;
Навстречу им она встает;
Свершилось: куплены три ночи,
И ложе смерти их зовет.

Благословенные жрецами,
Теперь из урны роковой
Пред неподвижными гостями
Выходят жребии чредой.
И первый — Флавий, воин смелый,
В дружинах римских поседелый;
Снести не мог он от жены
Высокомерного презренья;
Он принял вызов наслажденья,

Как принимал во дни войны
Он вызов ярого сраженья.
За ним Критон, младой мудрец,
Рожденный в рощах Эпикура,
Критон, поклонник и певец
Харит, Киприды и Амура...
Любезный сердцу и очам,
Как вешний цвет едва развитый,
Последний имени векам
Не передал. Его ланиты
Пух первый нежно отенял;
Восторг в очах его сиял:
Страстей неопытная сила
Кипела в сердце молодом...
И с умилением на нем
Царица взор остановила.

(IV, 386-89)

11. Пушкин, „Простишь ли мне ревнивые мечты" (p. 28).

Окружена поклонников толпой,
Зачем для всех казаться хочешь милой,
И всех дарит надеждою пустой
Твой чудный взор, то нежный, то унылый?
. . . . . .
Не видишь ты, когда, в толпе их страстной,
Беседы чужд, один и молчалив,
Терзаюсь я досадой одинокой. . .

(II, 161; 1823)

12. Пушкин, „Ангел" (pp. 29-30).

Дух отрицанья, дух сомненья
На духа чистого взирал
И жар невольный умиленья
Впервые смутно познавал.

„Прости, — он рек, — тебя я видел,
И ты недаром мне сиял:
Не все я в небе ненавидел,
Не все я в мире презирал".

(III, 17, 1827)

13. Пушкин, „К***'' (р. 30).

Я помню чудное мгновенье:
Передо мной явилась ты,
Как мимолетное виденье,
Как гений чистой красоты.

. . . . .

Шли годы. Бурь порыв мятежный
Рассеял прежние мечты,

. . . . .

Душе настало пробужденье:
И вот опять явилась ты,
Как мимолетное виденье,
Как гений чистой красоты.

И сердце бьется в упоенье,
И для него воскресли вновь
И божество, и вдохновенье,
И жизнь, и слезы, и любовь.

(II, 267, 1825)

14. Пушкин, 1824 (р. 30).

И чудо в пустыне тогда совершилось:
Минувшее в новой красе оживилось;

. . . . .

И чувствует путник и силу, и радость;
В крови заиграла воскресшая младость. . .

(II, 213, 1824)

15. Пушкин, „Полтава'' (р. 50).

И подлинно в Украйне нет
Красавицы Нат/алье/ равной

. . . . . .

Звездой горят ее глаза
Но редко в них видна слеза.
Зарей уста /у/ ней алеют
Но редко, редко и на миг
Улыбка оживляет их —
/Природа/ странно воспитала
Ей душу в тишине степей

И жертвой пламенных /страстей/
Судьба Нат/алью/ назначала

(J.V., 186-88)

16. Пушкин, „Евгений Онегин" (p. 52).

Беспечной прелестью мила,
Она сидела у стола
С блестящей Ниной Воронскою,
Сей Клеопатрою Невы;
И верно б согласилась вы,
Что Нина мраморной красою
Затмить соседку не могла,
Хоть ослепительна была.

(VIII, 16; 1830)

17. Пушкин, „Евгений Онегин" (p. 53).

И представительница света,
И та, чья скромная планета
Должна была когда-нибудь
Смиренным счастьем блеснуть,
И та, которой сердце, тайно
Нося безумной страсти казнь,
Питало ревность и боязнь, —
Соединенные случайно,
Друг дружке чуждые душой,
Сидели тут одна с другой.

(V, 554)

18. Пушкин, „Евгений Онегин" (p. 53).

Смотрите: в залу Нина входит,
Остановилась у дверей
И взгляд рассеянный обводит
Кругом внимательных гостей;
. . . .
И все в восторге, в небесах
Пред сей волшебною картиной. . .

(V, 556)

19. Пушкин, „Евгений Онегин" (р. 54).

Вечор сказала мне R. C.:
Давно желала я вас видеть.
Зачем? — мне говорили все,
Что я вас буду ненавидеть.
За что? — за резкий разговор,
За легкомысленное мненье
О всем; за колкое презренье
Ко всем; однако ж это вздор.
Вы надо мной смеяться властны,
Но вы совсем не так опасны;
И знали ль вы до сей поры,
Что просто — очень вы добры?

.   .   .   .

Вчера у В., оставя пир,
R. C. летела как зефир,

.   .   .   .

Я пред Венерою Невы
Толпу влюбленную раздвинул.

(V, 543-45)

20. Пушкин, „Евгений Онегин" (р. 55).

Но поздно. Тихо спит Одесса;
И бездыханна и тепла
Немая ночь. Луна взошла,
Прозрачно-легкая завеса
Объемлет небо. Все молчит;
Лишь море Черное шумит. . .

(V, 208)

21. Пушкин, „Клеопатра" (рр. 74-75).

То по водам седого Нила
Под тенью пышного ветрила
В своей триреме золотой
Плывет Кипридою младой.
Всечасно пред ее глазами
Пиры сменяются пирами,
И кто постиг в душе своей
Все таинства ее ночей? . .

155

Вотще! в ней сердце глухо страждет,
Оно утех безвестных жаждет —
Утомлена, пресыщена,
Больна бесчувствием она. . .

(VI, 605-06)

22. Пушкин, (р. 75).

Она, томясь тоскою, бродит
В своих садах; она заходит
В покои тайные дворца,
Где ключ угромого скопца
Хранит невольников прекрасных
И юношей стыдливо страстных

(VI, 740)

23. Пушкин, „К Вельможе" (р. 88).

       . . .За твой суровый пир
То чтитель промысла, то скептик, то безбожник,
Садился Дидерот на шаткий свой треножник,
Бросал парик, глаза в восторге закрывал
И проповедовал. И скромно ты внимал
За чашей медленной афею иль деисту,
Как любопытный скиф афинскому софисту.
.   .   .   .   .

          . . .Ступив за твой порог,
Я вдруг переношусь во дни Екатерины.
Книгохранилище, кумиры, и картины,
И стройные сады свидетельствуют мне,
Что благосклонствуешь ты музам в тишине,
.   .   .   .   .

Ты, не участвуя в волнениях мирских,
Порой насмешливо в окно глядишь на них
И видишь оборот во всем кругообразный.

Так, вихорь дел забыв для муз и неги праздной,
В тени порфирных бань и мраморных палат,
Вельможи римские встречали свой закат.
И к ним издалека то воин, то оратор,
То консул молодой, то сумрачный диктатор
Являлись день-другой роскошно отдохнуть,
Вздохнуть о пристани и вновь пуститься в путь.
(III, 169-71)

24. Пушкин, 1836 (p. 89).

Ценитель умстеннных творений исполинских,
Друг бардов английских, любовник муз латинских,
Ты к мощной древности опять меня манишь,
Ты снова мне. . . . . велишь.
Простясь с . . . . мечтой и бедным идеалом,
Я приготовился бороться с Ювеналом,
Чьи строгие стихи, неопытный поэт,
Стихами перевесть я было дал обет.
Но, развернув его суровые творенья,
Не мог я одолеть пугливого смущенья. . .
Стихи бесстыдные приапами торчат,
В них звуки странною гармонией трещат,
Картины . . . . . латинского разврата

. . . .

(III, 380)

25. Пушкин, „ Египетские ночи” (pp. 104-5).

„ . . . .
Предмет ничтожный поминутно
Тебя тревожит и манит.
Стремиться к небу должен гений,
Обязан истинный поэт
Для вдохновенных песнопений
Избрать возвышенный предмет.”
— Зачем крутится ветр в овраге,
Подъемлет лист и пыль несет,
Когда корабль в недвижной влаге
Его дыханья жадно ждет?
Зачем от гор и мимо башен
Летит орел, тяжел и страшен,
На чахлый пень? Спроси его.
Зачем арапа своего
Младая любит Дездемона,
Как месяц любит ночи мглу?
Затем, что ветру и орлу
И сердцу девы нет закона.
Таков поэт: как Аквилон,
Что хочет, то и носит он —
Орлу подобно, он летает
И, не спросясь ни у кого,

Как Дездемона избирает
Кумир для сердца своего.

(VI, 379-80)

26. Пушкин, „Поэт и толпа" (р. 109).

В разврате каменейте смело:
Не оживит вас лиры глас!
Душе противны вы, как гробы.

(III, 88)

27. Пушкин, „Ответ анониму" (рр. 111-12).

Смешон, участия кто требует у света!
Холодная толпа взирает на поэта,
Как на заезжего фигляра: если он
Глубоко выразит сердечный, тяжкий стон,
И выстраданный стих, пронзительно-унылый,
Ударит по сердцам с неведомою силой, —
Она в ладони бьет и хвалит, иль порой
Неблагосклонною кивает головой.

(III, 179)

28. Блок, „Клеопатра" (рр. 127-28).

Открыт паноптикум печальный
Один, другой и третий год.
Толпою пьяной и нахальной
Спешим. . . В гробу царица ждет.

Она лежит в гробу стеклянном,
И не мертва и не жива,
А люди шепчут неустанно
О ней бесстыдные слова,

Она раскинулась лениво —
Навек забыть, навек уснуть. . .
Змея легко, неторопливо
Ей жалит восковую грудь. . .

Я сам, позорный и продажный,
С кругами синими у глаз,
Пришел взглянуть на профиль важный,
На воск, открытый напоказ. . .

Тебя рассматривает каждый,
Но, если б гроб твой не был пуст,
Я услыхал бы не однажды
Надменный вздох истлевших уст:

„Кадите мне. Цветы рассыпьте.
Я в незапамятных веках
Была царицею в Египте.
Теперь — я воск. Я тлен. Я прах”. —

„Царица! Я пленен тобою!
Я был в Египте лишь рабом,
А ныне суждено судьбою
Мне быть поэтом и царем!

Ты видишь ли теперь из гроба,
Что Русь, как Рим, пьяна тобой?
Что я и Цезарь — будем оба
В веках равны перед судьбой?”

Замолк. Смотрю. Она не слышит.
Но грудь колышется едва
И за прозрачной тканью дышит. . .
И слышу тихие слова:

„Тогда я исторгала грозы.
Теперь исторгну жгучей всех
У пьяного поэта — слезы,
У пьяной проститутки — смех”.

1907

29. Ахматова, „Клеопатра"

I am air and fire...
Shakespeare

Александрийские чертоги
Покрыла сладостная тень.
Пушкин

Уже целовала Антония мертвые губы,
Уже на коленях пред Августом слезы лила...
И предали слуги. Грохочут победные трубы
Под римским орлом, и вечерняя стелется мгла.

И входит последний плененный ее красотою,
Высокий и статный, и шепчет в смятении он:
„Тебя — как рабыню... в триумфе пошлет пред собою..."
Но шеи лебяжей все так же спокоен наклон.

А завтра детей закуют. О, как мало осталось
Ей дела на свете — еще с мужиком пошутить
И черную змейку, как будто прощальную жалость,
На смуглую грудь равнодушной рукой положить.

1940